THE SHAKESPEARE FRAUD

THE POLITICS BEHIND THE PEN

By Ted Story

Edited by William Boyle

Forever Press
2016

D0841915

Published by

Forever Press
PO Box 263
Somerville MA 02143
www.foreverpress.org

ISBN: 978-0-9835027-9-1

Cover Image by Whitney Cookman

Images on pages viii, 19, 31, 54
92, 124 courtesy of WikiMedia Commons

Fig. 7 (p. 106), Southampton in the Tower, by permission
of His Grace the Duke of Buccleuch and Queensbury, K.T.

Fig. 4 (p. 45), Mary Browne, courtesy of Wikipedia.org

Printed in the USA

Dedication

To Cynthia
The love of my life
Who puts up with me

To Hank Whittemore
Who found the key and opened the door

TABLE OF CONTENTS

Fig. 1 - The Founder of the Fraud
(Robert Cecil)

INTRODUCTION

When I was ten years old I discovered that some people didn't think Shakespeare wrote Shakespeare and that other people were scandalized. I overheard my father mention Delia Bacon and her theory that Francis Bacon (no relative) was the real Shakespeare. Her book was in our bookcase. My father was an engineer and thought the idea of hidden codes was intriguing and there might be something to it. On the other hand...

I don't recall the subject coming up again for the next forty years, thirty of which I spent in the professional theatre. The writer, Shakespeare, seldom gets mentioned in professional theatre circles because we haven't found a way to connect the man and the work. It doesn't pay off, dramatically, so we mostly just pretend he's not there.

Then, one day, a producing partner of mine put a slim volume in my hand entitled *"The Man Who Was Shakespeare: A Summary of the Case unfolded in "The Mysterious William Shakespeare: The Myth and the Reality"* by Charlton Ogburn.

"What do you know about Shakespeare, the man?" he said.

Being an actor turned director turned producer and, feeling a little ignorant and trapped, I responded with the safe, theatrical answer I had heard so often:

"Not much—it's the work that's important," I replied.

"Read this," he said, "You'll learn a lot."

I did—and I did—and Shakespeare has been on my mind ever since. I devoured the slim volume and also the full size Ogburn book and Thomas Looney's book along with many others and became absolutely convinced that it was Edward de Vere, 17th Earl of Oxford who was the real Shakespeare. Why had I never heard of this before? How could all those college professors be so wrong? True— there was no "smoking gun"—the evidence was circumstantial, but there was a lot of it. It made good sense to me.

I also read up on the other major candidate, the man from Stratford, and I found that the argument for him is also circumstantial but boils down to just one item: His name is on the books! Well, not really his name, but a name very similar. His name in legal documents, including his will, is spelled variously Shaksper, Shakspere, Shakspe and Shagspere, whereas the name on the books is always spelled "Shakespeare" or sometimes "Shake-speare" with a hyphen. The similarity of his real name to the name on the books is the best there is for verifiable facts that connect the Stratford man to the works. If there is anything else, I haven't heard of it.

For the sake of clarity, because this is all about confusion over a name, when I refer to the actual author, whoever he may be, I will spell his name "Shakespeare" or "Shake-speare" (authorial spelling). When I'm referring to the man from Stratford, I will spell his name "Shagspere."

Does it matter? Ogburn said: "It matters a great deal to those who consider his works to be Western man's highest achievement in literature. It seems a question of elementary justice that the man responsible for this tremendous achievement should receive the credit for it." It also seems to me that if the "experts" ever open their eyes and see what's staring them in the face, it will open up a treasure trove of research and discovery. It would become a jobs program in Literature and History departments all over the English speaking world.

THE SHAKESPEARE FRAUD

Who was Shakespeare? The traditional academic and popular favorite is the Man from Stratford, but doubt is growing. The more honest answer is that we're not sure. Hundreds, perhaps thousands, of books have been written to try to make a plausible case that the man from Stratford actually wrote the Works of Shakespeare but, so far, no one has succeeded.

Astonishingly, in four hundred years no one has ever been able to absolutely connect him with <u>any</u> written words except for six dissimilar signatures on legal documents, three of which are on his will, which mentions no books or other writings. He left most of his estate to his two illiterate daughters (hard to believe but, yes, they really were) and, for reasons much speculated on, he left his "2nd best bed" to his wife of 34 years. No one in his hometown of Stratford ever spoke of him as a writer and nothing has ever been found that connects him or his life to the writings. Most damning of all, no one has been able to come up with a plausible, coherent story that would explain how this young man, probably possessing only a rudimentary education and no entré to the movers and shakers of the Elizabethan world, could possibly have grown up and written the soaring poetry and the sophisticated political plays betraying an insiders' knowledge of the workings of the court, credited to someone named William Shakespeare. His doubtful education, his work as a loan shark, his hoarding of grain in a famine and his propensity for suing people for small amounts of money are difficult to reconcile with the refined sensibility, empathy towards other men and disdainful attitude towards money displayed in the works. (*"He who steals my purse steals trash, 'tis something, nothing."*—Othello)

There is no logical, coherent story that leads us step by step from his youth in Stratford-on-`Avon to fame in

London as an actor/playwright, making himself wealthy in the process. Aside from the famous "missing years" of 1585-1592, for which we know nothing at all, what we do have is a few records of money lending, dealing in commodities and owning property. We also know where he is buried. Well, almost. We're not sure whether Shagspere is in the wall or the floor of Trinity Church in Stratford, but I'm sure he's there somewhere—everyone says so. However, 400 years of digging for clues has failed to turn up a logical story of how that man buried in Trinity Church became the man that most experts claim is the author of the greatest body of work in the English language. I agree with Henry James who famously said, "I am 'sort of haunted' by the conviction that the divine William is the biggest and most successful fraud ever practiced on a patient world." To put it bluntly, I believe the experts are wrong. I believe that Edward de Vere, 17th Earl of Oxford is the real writer.

In 1987 three US Supreme Court justices; Brennan, Blackman and Stevens, held a televised moot court debate over who was the actual author of the plays, Shagspere or Oxford. Although the verdict went to Shagspere, solely on the grounds of the longevity of his claim, Justice Stevens closed the proceedings with a wise observation that no one has followed through on:

"... in my opinion the strongest theory of the case requires an assumption, for some reason we don't understand, that the Queen and her Prime Minister decided, 'We want this man to be writing plays under a pseudonym'. Of course, this thesis may be so improbable that it is not worth even thinking about; but I would think that the Oxfordians really have not yet put together a concise, coherent theory that they are prepared to defend, in all respects."

4

At parties, hearing of my iconoclastic beliefs, people seek me out and ask me to tell them my story of Shakespeare, which I'm happy to do. I try to give them a cocktail party length answer. Unfortunately, I always fail because, as I have found out, this story is too long for a cocktail party and too complicated to explain after one Martini.

My longtime personal and professional relationships with living playwrights have taught me that if a play is any good it will be rooted somewhere in the author's psyche and, frequently, in his biography. As Oscar Wilde said, "Every portrait painted with feeling is a portrait of the artist, not the sitter." Think of Eugene O'Neill, Tennessee Williams, Arthur Miller, Edward Albee and Sam Shepard. Playwrights usually don't like to talk about these connections but they all agree they are there.

My belief that Edward de Vere, 17th Earl of Oxford (usually referred to as just "Oxford") wrote the works seems well-grounded and logical to me, partly because his personal history seems to be reflected over and over again in the plays. To begin with, he spent over a year travelling in Italy where several Shakespeare plays take place. He, like Hamlet, is waylaid by pirates and is left naked on the shore. Polonius, the Secretary of State of Denmark and his daughter bear a remarkable resemblance to Oxford's father-in-law, Lord Burghley, Queen Elizabeth's Principal Secretary, in whose home he grew up and whose daughter he married and who actually had a list of precepts he gave to his son before he went abroad (like Polonius gives to Laertes). Like Timon of Athens, Oxford loses a fortune and becomes an outcast. He also has a wife he believes has cheated on him only to realize too late, like Othello, that he has been lied to by political enemies. His girlfriend's family declares open warfare against his men in the streets of London. One of them is killed like Mercutio is killed by Tybalt. He also has a brother-in-law who is sent to the Danish Court as an Ambassador by Queen Elizabeth who brings back stories of life in Denmark which show up in HAMLET. In play after play, Oxford's real life is fodder for Shakespeare's dramas.

Oxford also seems to have the right personality, the right knowledge and the right connections to be the author of Shakespeare's Works. But here, also, there is no "smoking gun" to absolutely pin it on him and, more importantly, there also is no complete story, no narrative, to logically bring us from Oxford, the young aristocratic prodigy, to Oxford, the man, walling himself up behind the pen-name of Shakespeare, claiming that his own name will be buried where his body is (the burial place of Oxford's remains is unknown) and that no one will ever know who really belongs to the name "William Shakespeare."

Oxford, like Hamlet, also had a close male friend named Horatio (his cousin, one half of the famous "Fighting Veres") whom Hamlet begs just before he dies:

O God, Horatio, what a wounded name,
Things standing thus unknown, shall leave behind me!
If thou didst ever hold me in thy heart,
Absent thee from felicity a while,
And in this harsh world draw thy breath in pain
To tell my story.

Horatio is long-since dead but, whenever I think of Hamlet, I think he's talking to me. Believing that the world has it very wrong, I feel a responsibility to help rediscover the truth of Shakespeare's story and to tell it as best I can.

Many of my fellow Oxfordians (people who believe that the 17th Earl of Oxford is Shakespeare) will tell you that the reason Oxford wrote plays under the pen-name of Shakespeare is that it would have been forbidden for Oxford, as a nobleman, to be known to write for the stage. That's true as far as it goes. A poet was an artist so a little poetry was OK for an artistic aristocrat but a playwright was considered to be a craftsman—he made something. Wheelwrights made wheels and playwrights made plays. We theatre professionals still think of ourselves as craftsmen. The word "build" is ubiquitous in the language of theatre. We don't speak of "sewing" costumes, we "build" them. We talk all the time of "building" a light cue, "building" a scene or "building" a dramatic climax. And, of course, we build sets. Being a craftsman was forbidden to the aristocratic class in the 16th Century. But It still seemed to me that the enormous effort required to keep Oxford's secret for four centuries was out of proportion to the relatively minor problem of one more aristocrat covering up his socially unacceptable pastime of writing for the stage, particularly since it was customary for other hidden aristocratic writers to arrange to "come out of the closet" after death. There had to be another, much more important, reason for the mystery surrounding Mr. Shakespeare.

Then, in 2005, Hank Whittemore wrote *The Monument,* his groundbreaking study of SHAKE-SPEARES SONNETS of 1609, showing them to be, not just a collection of love poems, but a political diary recording the existence of a Tudor Prince who should have succeeded Elizabeth as King Henry IX but, instead, was held in the Tower of London until her death and King James VI, of Scotland, was safely on the throne of England. Royal succession! Finally, here was a cause sufficient to justify the concealment effort required to last 400 years along with a logical story—at least a part of it. It tells us that Oxford wrote the Sonnets and that he wrote them to the 3rd Earl of

Southampton, his son, in order to immortalize his right to the throne in a monument of (apparently) romantic poetry.

From Sonnet 81:

Your monument shall be my gentle verse,
Which eyes not yet created shall o'er-read;
And tongues to be your being shall rehearse,
When all the breathers of this world are dead;
You still shall live, such virtue hath my pen,
Where breath most breathes, even in the mouths of men.

He knows how good a writer he is.

Trying to demonstrate this to a non-academic audience, Hank and I wrote a 90 minute one-man presentation based on his book, with him starring, and named it *Shakespeare's Treason*, since the Sonnets' claim of the existence of a Tudor prince was an act of treason. We've had the honor of presenting it live at The Globe Theatre in London where the uber-Stratfordian, James Shapiro, saw it and gave it what I consider to be a rave review in his well-received book, *Contested Will*:

"It was a spellbinding performance, as perfect a marriage of conspiratorial history and autobiographical analysis as one could imagine. If the enthusiastic response of the audience that evening was any indication, Oxfordian concerns about the riskiness of Whittemore's approach were misplaced. I looked around the room and saw the same kind of people— middle-aged, sensibly dressed, middle-class—who regularly attend lectures about Shakespeare, nodding their heads in agreement and laughing aloud at the funny parts. I found it all both impressive and demoralizing ......"

We've recently made a DVD of *Shake-speare's*

Treason. It goes a long way in telling the story of a man trapped into giving up his blood-right claim to the throne of England in order that he might live on and keep a cause alive. It also provides an historical time, place and purpose for the relationship of Henry Wriothesley, 3rd Earl of Southampton and the author, pen-named "Shakespeare." However, in only 90 minutes it leaves many questions unanswered. It was impossible to paint a complete picture of how it all happened and of the many people involved and their many cross-motives that finally resulted in "Shakespeare," the man and the myth.

When it comes to Elizabethan History, what we know is what that master of political deceit, Robert Cecil, wants us to know. Robert Cecil, the hunchbacked son of Lord Burghley, was the power behind the throne at the end of Queen Elizabeth's reign and continued on into James's reign. Using his control over the tools of history (total access to government files and libraries and other writers willing to write to order, not to mention a large furnace) he created what is perhaps the greatest fraud the world has ever seen, certainly one of the longest-lived, in order to protect a very dangerous state secret from being known. As Napoleon said, "History is a myth that men agree to believe." George Orwell added that, "History is written by the winners." Well then, who were the winners and who were the losers and what was that state secret? This is what the story of Shakespeare is really about.

Full disclaimer—I'm not an historian and what follows is not history—it's a story—the true story of Shakespeare as I see it.

My life has been spent in the theatre telling stories. Telling a story on the stage is very much about finding out how one discrete event or scene in a play connects to another event and then to another and another to make a complete story arc which ends at the final curtain. It's the way the events are joined together that make the story.

Trying to discover Shakespeare's story exposed me to so many facts and contemporary comments on so many topics it made my head spin. In my attempt to make order out of chaos, I started putting the factual tidbits I was learning into a long timeline. That made everything a little clearer, but I still couldn't find a beginning, middle or end. I couldn't even decide who the main character was. I finally tried grouping the timeline by character and following the arc of each character separately from the other characters. Suddenly it was clear why I had been having such trouble. I was looking at a dozen major characters with more than a dozen overlapping storylines struggling to live out their individual ambitions and entangling themselves in each others' lives while doing so. No wonder I couldn't explain it at a cocktail party!

Until now, no one has proposed a complete, logical and possible story for any Shakespeare candidate showing how the important pieces fit together. I don't claim that my story is totally true. As I said, this is not history. But I do claim that it is totally logical and totally possible and, therefore, possibly true. (For the record: I believe it is true.) We have to try to create Justice Stevens' "coherent theory" of Shakespeare and his motives if we are ever to understand his life and work. This story makes sense to me and does not violate anything I believe to be true. If you will do me the theatrical favor of willingly suspending your disbelief (only for a short time) I hope it will make sense to you too. My method is to arrange the individual factoids gleaned from the research of others into several separate timelines and to "tell the story" which I think connects them. So, for each chapter I've made a list of factoids followed by the story I believe connects them.

Since I believe that the 17th Earl of Oxford is the man who created and wrote under the pen name "William Shakespeare" it seems appropriate to include quotations from his written works when they seem germane.

I'll begin with the engine which drives the whole story—The Tudor Dynasty. Without the Tudor Dynasty and Henry VIII, there would be no Shakespeare.

But first—you can't tell the players without a scorecard.

CAST OF CHARACTERS

In the beginning I had trouble keeping the names straight (some have several) so I've included a list of the main ones for your reference:

HENRY TUDOR: HENRY VIII, Tudor King of England from 1509-1547.

EDWARD TUDOR: Henry's son; Edward VI; Child king of England 1547-1553.

MARY TUDOR: Henry's first daughter; "Bloody Mary," Queen of England 1553-1558.

ELIZABETH TUDOR: Henry's second daughter; "The Virgin Queen," "Bess," "Gloriana," Queen Elizabeth I 1558-1603

ROBERT DUDLEY: Earl of Leicester; "Robin"; Queen Elizabeth's "favorite" and thought by many to be her lover. Infamous for his reputed use of poison.

ROBERT DEVEREAU: 2nd Earl of Essex; "Essex"; Robert Dudley's stepson and protégée. Replaced Dudley as Elizabeth's "favorite." Executed for leading the Essex Rebellion.

WILLIAM CECIL: Lord Burghley; (Born a commoner, Elizabeth raised him up to the aristocracy). Elizabeth's Principal Secretary & chief advisor.

ROBERT CECIL: William's son who took over his father's position. Known for his hunchback and his Machiavellian mind.

ANNE CECIL: William Cecil's daughter, married to Edward de Vere.

EDWARD DE VERE: Edward Oxenford; 17th Earl of Oxford, the oldest noble family in England, going back to William the Conqueror; "Oxford"; Spent his early life living with William Cecil as a ward of the court. Married Anne Cecil. I believe he wrote the works.

HENRY WRIOTHESLEY (pronounced: "Rizley"): 2nd Earl of Southampton; Disloyal Catholic Lord of a large estate in southern England.

HENRY WRIOTHESLEY: 3rd Earl of Southampton; Officially, the son of the 2nd Earl. I believe he was actually the Tudor Prince son of Queen Elizabeth and Edward de Vere, raised by the 2nd Earl as his offspring (a "changling child").

JOHN SHAGSPERE: A glover, wool dealer and loan shark living in Stratford-on-Avon. Politically rises to level of Mayor.

WILLIAM SHAGSPERE: John's son; brogger (illegal broker/dealer of raw wool) and loan shark. His real name was close enough to Oxford's pen-name that Robert Cecil put him on the payroll and claimed that he was William Shakespeare, the playwright.

CHAPTER 1

MY KINGDOM FOR A TUDOR HEIR

THE TIMELINE

February 1516: After five miscarriages and infant deaths, Henry VIII & 1st wife, Catherine of Aragon, produce a daughter, Mary Tudor.

June 1519: Desperately wanting a son and heir, Henry sires a bastard with Elizabeth Blount and names him Henry FitzRoy (Henry, Son of the King)

June 1525: Henry FitzRoy (6 yrs old) is raised up to the aristocracy, made Duke of Richmond and a Knight of the Garter.

September 1533: Still desperate for a legitimate son, Henry breaks with the Catholic Church and makes England Protestant in order to annul his marriage to Catherine and marries Anne Boleyn. Anne gives birth to a girl, destined to become Elizabeth I.

May 1536: Two miscarriages later and still trying for a legitimate son to inherit the Tudor throne, Henry VIII executes Anne Boleyn and marries Jane Seymour.

July 1536: Henry VIII's 2nd Act of Succession, in which Parliament gave Henry the right to decide his own successors, de-legitimizes Elizabeth and her older half-sister Mary and they both become, legally speaking, bastards.

July 1536: Henry FitzRoy dies.

October 1537: Edward VI is born to Henry and Jane Seymour but he is a sickly boy. Jane dies shortly after.

1540: Henry marries Ann of Cleves and annuls it after six months. He complains that she is homely and smells and never consummates the marriage.

1540: Henry marries Catherine Howard. He beheads her for being unfaithful.

1543: Henry marries Catherine Parr. She survives him.

July 1543: With his own death not far off and his only son a sickly boy, the future of the Tudor Dynasty is uncertain. Henry VIII's 3rd Act of Succession is passed, which returns both Mary and Elizabeth to the line of succession behind Prince Edward. However, they both remain, officially, bastards.

January 1547: Henry VIII dies and Edward VI becomes King at age 10.

July 1553: Six years later King Edward VI dies, childless, at age 16 after nominating Protestant Lady Jane Grey as successor to the Crown in his will, thus subverting the claim of his Catholic half-sister Mary.

Mary Tudor asserts her blood right under Henry's Third Succession Act and she becomes Queen (Lady Grey, the "nine day queen," is executed). She legitimizes herself (being a bastard doesn't seem to be a problem when you're queen) and marries Phillip II of Spain. England will be Catholic again and Mary wastes no time introducing the Inquisition to England and earning the sobriquet, "Bloody Mary."

November 1558: Five years later, after a false pregnancy, Mary dies and Elizabeth is crowned Queen at age 25. She does not legitimize herself. I guess bastardy isn't what it used to be. As Lord Great Chamberlain, the 16th Earl of Oxford officiates at her coronation. England will become Protestant again.

THE STORY

One thing is certain: Nothing is more important to King Henry VIII than to have a son of his own blood to carry on the Tudor dynasty after his death. He is willing to do just about anything to make it happen, including separating England from the Catholic Church and becoming a wife-beheading monster, not to mention fathering a bastard son to be his heir in case all else fails. Nothing works and he dies leaving a sickly boy on the throne and two girls waiting in the wings.

With Edward VI and Mary ahead of her in succession and abundant plots against her life, the odds of Elizabeth ever becoming Queen are small. However, after cleverly surviving the reigns of her father, her half brother and her half-sister, all of whom had procreation problems, she is now the *last of the Tudors* and it is completely in her hands as to whether the Tudor family dynasty will continue.

CHAPTER 2

GET MARRIED, BESS!

THE TIMELINE

January 1559: The House of Commons petitions the Queen to marry and produce an heir. The Queen instructs them that, as befits an absolute monarch, this is between herself and God and therefore is none of their business.

June 1559: The Spanish ambassador, De Feria, reports to Prince Phillip, Elizabeth's ex-brother-in-law, now back in Spain, *"She is a very vain and clever woman. She must have been thoroughly schooled in the manner in which her father conducted his affairs. She is determined to be governed by no one."* He went on, *"She is incomparably more feared than her sister, and gives her orders and has her way as absolutely as her father did."*

June 1559: In the summer of 1559, gossip is rife that the Queen is with child or has already had children by Robert Dudley, her "favorite."

September 1560: Robert Dudley's wife, Amy Robsart, dies amid rumors that he murdered her to free himself up to marry the Queen. He denies it but the rumors persist and make a royal marriage impossible, even if Elizabeth had wanted to, which I doubt.

July 1561: There are new rumors of a child by Elizabeth and Dudley. "She looks like one lately come out of childbed," says the Duchess of Suffolk

August 1561: The Queen visits Castle Hedingham for five days to visit her Lord Great Chamberlain, the 16th Earl of Oxford, highest ranking nobleman in England, who officiated at her coronation. While there, she is charmed by young Edward de Vere, the future 17th Earl of Oxford. She is 28, beautiful and smart. He is 11 and precocious.

August 1562: A year later the 16th Earl of Oxford dies at age 51. By law, his son, Edward de Vere, (now the 17th Earl, age 12) becomes a royal ward of the Queen and leaves home for London, looking mournfully regal, at the head of 140 men on horseback dressed in black livery, to live in the home of, and be educated by, William Cecil, the future Lord Burghley, Elizabeth's Principal Secretary.

October 1562: Elizabeth falls ill with smallpox. Everyone thinks she may die. Shockingly, she wants Dudley made Protector of the Realm if she dies.

November 1563: Fresh from her smallpox scare, the House of Lords petitions the Queen to marry and produce an heir. "It please your majesty to dispose yourself to marry, where you will, with whom you will, and as shortly as you will." In a fury, Elizabeth prorogues Parliament (discontinues without dissolving) until 1566, when she needs money.

May 1570: Pope Pius V, following up on his previous request to English Catholics to assassinate Queen Elizabeth, excommunicates her and releases English Catholics from their obligation to obey her.

THE STORY

Elizabeth has a responsibility to her Tudor ancestors and to her country to provide an heir to succeed her. An heir seems to require a husband and everyone, from her Privy Council to Parliament to the people on the streets, want her to get married. However, she's wise to the ways of the patriarchal Tudor world and is determined never to

Fig. 2 - A young Queen
Elizabeth, circa 1570s

marry. She knows that a husband would get the real power and any children would become the focus of plots against her. She also knows that the only way for a woman to stay alive and succeed as an absolute ruler is to remain unmarried and emulate a strong male like her father, Henry VIII. He is her role model and, according to the Spanish Ambassador, she has learned her lessons well. Her determination to rule by divine right and not share power with anyone brings her into immediate conflict with Parliament and with the English public. They expect her to do what Queens are expected to do: provide for a peaceful royal transition to the next generation by marrying and bearing a child, preferably a boy. The War of the Roses is legendary—Henry Tudor brought domestic peace to war-weary England by joining the White Rose and the Red through marriage and procreation. This peace has now lasted over 70 years. It's what the Tudors are known for. All of England expects her to do her duty, but she rudely reminds Parliament who is Queen. Four years into her reign, she almost dies from smallpox, and her frightened subjects and Parliament increase the pressure to provide an heir.

And if that weren't enough, the Pope has made killing the Queen seem like a holy act to England's Catholic population, and therefore an heir seems all the more necessary.

CHAPTER 3

THE CECILS

THE TIMELINE

September 1521: William Cecil is born to an innkeeper.

1535: He enters Cambridge, at the time a hotbed of Protestant thinking.

January 1541: He marries Mary Cheke, daughter of a Cambridge professor.

1542: Son and heir, Thomas Cecil is born.

January 1543: Mary Cheke dies.

1546: William marries Mildred Cooke, whose father is a leading supporter of the Reformation.

1548: Edward VI becomes a child king and his uncle, Edward Seymour, 1st Duke of Somerset, becomes his Protector. William Cecil becomes Protector Somerset's personal secretary.

1550: Somerset is overthrown by John Dudley, Earl of Warwick, in a coup and Cecil becomes Secretary of State to Dudley.

1551: Cecil is knighted and granted several estates.

1553: Edward VI dies and Lady Jane Grey comes to the throne for nine days before Mary asserts her Tudor blood-right and takes the crown for herself. Cecil lays low while Mary is Queen.

November 1558: Mary dies after a false pregnancy. Elizabeth becomes Queen and appoints William Cecil Principal Secretary and Privy Counselor.

1562: Cecil House, a magnificent structure, containing one of the largest private libraries in the world, just steps from the palace, is finished at the same time young Oxford is beginning his nine-year stay to be educated by William Cecil as a ward of the court.

June 1563: Second son Robert Cecil is born.

February 1571: The Queen elevates William Cecil to the Aristocracy as Baron Burghley. He is also elected Chancellor of Cambridge University.

July 1571: William Cecil (now Lord Burghley) holds an engagement party for his now ex-ward, Edward de Vere, now 17th Earl of Oxford, and his daughter, Anne.

1572: Burghley is made a Knight of the Garter and also Lord Treasurer. He is now the most powerful man in government.

1573: It is reported that *"Secretary Cecil may be called the King of England."* [Calendar of Papal State Papers, Memorial of the Affairs of the Netherlands and the Queen of Scotts, by Sir Thomas Stucley 1573].

THE STORY

History has painted William Cecil as a dull but faithful servant, loyal, patriotic and bureaucratically skilled. His contemporaries acknowledged him as the virtual Ruler of England during Elizabeth's reign. The truth is that he was both. He had amazing survival skills and rose through a succession of politically dangerous situations, ending up serving a firebrand of a Queen who is determined to reign as absolutely as her notorious father. William Cecil (soon to be Baron Burghley) makes that possible and, in the process, guides England through the great Protestant revolution of the 16th Century, including the defeat of the Spanish Armada.

He's a very ambitious man from the tradesman's background of his father, an innkeeper. He graduates from Cambridge and contracts a fortuitous marriage to the daughter of John Cheke who will become tutor to the child-King, Edward VI, whose Protector is Lord Somerset. This connection eventually leads to Cecil becoming Somerset's personal secretary. Somerset is overthrown in a coup by John Dudley, Earl of Warwick, who makes William Cecil Secretary of State. Cecil arranges for the execution of Somerset and is knighted and granted a large number of estates as a reward. Like a chameleon, he survives the aborted reign of Lady Jane Grey and bends himself into a religious pretzel in order to survive with Catholic Queen Mary. On becoming Queen, Elizabeth's first appointment is William Cecil as Principal Secretary and a Privy Counselor. It's the most important decision of her reign. She doesn't want a husband but she needs William Cecil.

This brief history shows a smart, ambitious, self-made man who possesses unusual skills of self-preservation and political maneuvering. While loyally serving Elizabeth and

23

England he also manages to serve his own interests and acquires several estates and two enormous mansions filled with priceless treasures. He accumulates so much power that by 1573, in an official Vatican file, it is reported that *he, effectively, is the King of England*. If Cecil is good for England, he is even better for the Cecil family.

However, the success of the Cecils as the power behind the throne is locked to the success of the Tudors and the Queen can be difficult and irrational when it comes to marriage. It's his job to make sure the Tudors hold on to the crown of England. If he succeeds, the Cecils and the Tudors will be inextricably locked together in a permanent partnership, and he can leave a lasting legacy to ten year-old Robert, his non-inheriting 2nd son, born with a severe hunchback but with a steel-trap Machiavellian mind. William Cecil would like to found a dynasty of his own which would be the permanent power behind the Tudors. *But how can he preserve the Tudor Dynasty when the last of the Tudors won't marry?*

CHAPTER 4

HOW DOES A QUEEN WITHOUT A HUSBAND PRODUCE AN HEIR? OR ... WILLIAM CECIL'S "OTHER MEANS"

THE TIMELINE

January 1566: Following his superb education in Cecil House, Edward de Vere, the 17th Earl of Oxford, now 16 years old, receives the degree of Master of Arts from Cambridge.

February 1567: Oxford is admitted to Gray's Inn to study law.

1569: The French ambassador reports back to Paris that English nobles are convinced that Elizabeth will never marry, and *William Cecil is seeking "other means" to solve the succession crisis.* (Haigh p17, emphasis mine).

February 1571: William Cecil is raised up to the aristocracy by Queen Elizabeth and given the title Baron Burghley. He is also elected Chancellor of Cambridge University.

February 1571: Lord Burghley is made a Knight of the Garter and also Lord Treasurer. He has become the most powerful man in England.

April 1571: Oxford turns 21, leaves wardship and enters the House of Lords.

April 1571: Oxford becomes a serious candidate for Knight of the Garter, the highest order in England, garnering a first-place vote from all ten electors. They seem to think there's something very special about him.

April 1571: Parliament changes an old law regarding publicly speaking of any possible offspring of the Queen: They change the phrase *"Legal Issue* of the Queen's body" to *"Natural issue* of the Queen's body," which seems to permit people to discuss, publically, the possibility of a bastard heir to the throne without risking arrest for treason.

May 1571: Lord Oxford in Crimson velvet wins in the tiltyard for the Queen—"I'll be your champion." The queen presents him with a "tablet of diamonds." The Earl of Rutland writes; *"There is no man of life and agility in every respect in the Court but the Earl of Oxford"*

July 1571: William Cecil, Elizabeth's Principal Secretary and Oxford's warden, arranges for Oxford to get engaged to Anne Cecil, his 15 year-old daughter. The Queen seems pleased.

December 1571: Oxford marries Anne Cecil.

Jan 1573: John Pool writes to his father, *"The Queen wooed the Earl of Oxford but he would not fall in."*

May 1573: Five months later, Gilbert Talbot reports to his father about Oxford and Elizabeth. *"My Lord of Oxford is lately grown into great credit, for the Queen's Majesty delighteth more in his personage and his dancing and his valiantness than any other."* He continues that Oxford's father-in-law, the Great Burghley, *"winketh at all these love matters and will not meddle in any way."*

Mary Queen of Scots spells it out in a scathing letter to Elizabeth, her cousin, accusing her directly: "Even the Count of Oxford dared not cohabit with his wife for fear of losing the favor which he hoped to receive by becoming your lover."

THE STORY

Coming to London as a ward of the Queen to live in the home of the most powerful man in England , just a short walk from the palace, must have been exciting for young Edward de Vere. He was precocious and probably soaked up knowledge like a sponge in those heady surroundings and, as the highest ranking Earl in England (17th inheritor of the title), he had every reason to expect that he was destined for greatness. Edward was exposed to the best of everything including expert tutelage, supervised by Cecil and his wife, Mildred Cooke, possibly the most educated woman in England, and his maternal uncle, Arthur Golding, translator of Ovid's "Metamorphoses," the source of so many of the plays by Shakespeare, whoever he may be. William Cecil's library was one of the largest in the world and he employed world-renowned architects, gardeners and librarians to build and care for his ever-growing estate. Oxford is right there in the middle of it all. The superior education and training at Cecil house is followed by the best philosophy, critical thinking and law that Cambridge, Oxford and Gray's Inn can provide. Young Edward, an admitted prodigy, encouraged by Elizabeth, excels in everything he attempts: Music, astronomy, poetry, drama, horsemanship, jousting, history, law, botany, fashion, falconry, the Bible...The list goes on and on.

Now an adult at 21, he leaves wardship and takes his place in the House of Lords. As is customary, a marriage is arranged by his guardian, William Cecil. Cecil chooses his own daughter, Anne Cecil, who has grown up in his house with Edward, like a kid sister, and is now 15. Edward later claims the marriage was never consummated. Elizabeth elevates Cecil to become Baron Burghley and it appears, by the timing, that she may have done so in order that the marriage to his daughter not disparage Oxford's title (He can't be forced to marry beneath his station.).

As a political marriage, it bonds together the highest branch of the English Aristocracy (largely Catholic) with the head of England's rising Protestant government bureaucracy. But it also serves another, hitherto unnoticed, purpose. The marriage removes the newest, handsomest, richest, most eligible bachelor in Elizabeth's Court from female attention and permits Elizabeth to have a free hand. It becomes obvious to those present at court that she has her eye on Edward, in spite of his marriage to Anne. Imagine this red-haired, radiant goddess of a monarch, one of the most striking personalities in all Europe, flirting in front of the whole Court with the now-married twenty-three year-old Earl of Oxford. No wonder young Gilbert Talbot wrote to his father about it, saying, Lord Burghley "winketh at all these love matters and will not meddle in any way."

Elizabeth, almost forty, can hear her dynastic clock ticking and, apparently, has decided to solve her heir problem by taking a page from her father's book. She will have a "FitzRoy" of her own but, since she's a woman, she will have to keep him hidden away until a propitious moment long in the future. That way, she can fulfill her obligations to her people and to the Tudor dynasty and won't risk losing her power to a husband or to a power base surrounding a child. She can have her cake and eat it too! She will choose the proper father and Burghley will handle the gritty details. At some yet-to-be-determined date in the future, she and her chief advisor will triumphantly announce the existence of an heir of her blood who will succeed her. When? That's a future decision, which is the kind Elizabeth likes best.

In spite of the fact that Oxford is his son-in-law, Burghley looks the other way because, if he can facilitate the Queen's dynastic plans, the Tudors and the Cecils will be locked together and the Cecils will continue to be the power behind the throne for generations. Perhaps, some day, even *on* the throne. It apparently doesn't bother him that he has made his own daughter an unsuspecting pawn in this dynastic game because, after all, in Elizabethan England, aristocratic women are expected to be pawns in the political games of the men. The Tudor Dynasty itself is the result of such a marriage.

Since the Queen is one of the smartest and best-educated women in England and quite proud of it, it isn't surprising that she chooses the smartest and best-educated man. It doesn't hurt that he is also young, handsome, a fabulous competitive athlete in the tilt yard and comes from one of the oldest Norman families who came over even before William the Conqueror. And he makes her laugh. She chooses Edward de Vere, the 17th Earl of Oxford, who is now a ripe 23 to mate with her more mature, but still attractive, 39 years. This is not some accidental romance—this is carefully planned.

Among his fellow young lords, Oxford looks like he has a bright future because in 1571, having just turned 21, he receives 10 first place votes to be given the highest possible honor of becoming a Knight of the Garter. The Queen quashes it. She has other plans for young Oxford, and they don't involve making him politically more visible.

Why would Oxford agree to be part of this scheme? A difficult question to answer with any assurance but I think we must give some thought to it because, from what I know about Oxford, if he didn't believe in it, he wouldn't have done it.

Elizabeth's father, Henry VIII, was a warrior. He surrounded himself with other warriors and that was the kind of kingdom he ran. Elizabeth is not a warrior. She's a highly educated, cultured woman who speaks six languages and can read Latin and Greek. She loves music and plays the Lute and the Virginal. She also loves to dance and encourages artists and artisans. Her reign ends up being known as "The Golden Age." She doesn't want a husband but is looking for more than just a stud. What she's looking for is someone to help her lift England from it's position as a second rate cultural backwater, looked down on by the more sophisticated and cultured French and Italians. (The English weren't even using forks yet—they still ate with their daggers!). She dreams of a different England: powerful, literate and cultured. She needs a highly cultured man with good genes and a good heritage who is fun to be with (she loves to be entertained) and who can be trusted absolutely to keep a dynastic secret. She's looking for a partnership, not a marriage.

Oxford is from the oldest and most respected aristocratic family in England (by heredity, the Lord Great Chamberlain) and needs a way to be special and important to himself and to England. Like every young nobleman at court, his life is focused on pleasing Elizabeth, the "Goddess Queen." Unlike the other young nobles, he's a

Fig. 3 - The Welbeck portrait of Oxford, painted while he was in Paris (circa 1575-1576)

polymath with a romantic, poetic soul who needs a grand purpose in life in order to feel alive. I suspect that the Queen lured him with the promise of becoming the "Father of his Country." Not a king himself, but the father of a long line of kings (Like Banquo). He also needs an outlet for his insatiable need to write and tell stories. So, she would put his special talents to work by giving him a secret position, practically a separate branch of government, never before conceived of and reporting directly to her; something like a Minister of Culture, charged with bringing The

Renaissance to England. She wants their child to reign over a strong, cultured and respected country.

Oxford alludes to this function occasionally in letters to Burghley as being "about the Queen's business" and "I work for the Queen." Judging by his writing, she must also, as a sign of his position and of her trust, have given him a perpetual exemption from censorship. This looks like a perfect meshing of life goals for both of them.

Also, the sheer audaciousness of the plan must appeal to his dramatic sense. Imagine—to birth and raise a prince in secret, right under the court's nose! A great plot for a great cause—the Glory of England and the Tudor dynasty! And his son will be the dynastic Tudor king! He himself will be the father of a long line of Tudor kings. It's a hard offer to turn down. It will also guarantee him a very special relationship with the Queen of England and with England itself.

It appears to me that Elizabeth enters into this arrangement as an act of State (possibly even a secret marriage) for the benefit of England, the English people and the Tudor dynasty. When she said, "I am married to England," she really meant it. She has decided to bear an heir for England because England needs an heir and it's her duty as Tudor Queen to provide one. But she'll do it on her terms.

Shocking? When it comes to dynasties, there is no rulebook.

CHAPTER 5

WHAT IS THE TIMING OF THE BABY?

THE TIMELINE

January 1573: Elizabeth visits Matthew Parker who had been her mother's close advisor and is her Archbishop of Canterbury. Oxford accompanies her.

July 1573: She visits Parker a 2nd time.

September 1573: Elizabeth spends her 40th birthday with the Archbishop, then she drops from public view for six months.

March 1574: She visits Parker a fourth time, again with Oxford in tow.

April-May 1574: She continues her seclusion (nine months total). A court member reports, "The Queen's Majesty hath been melancholy disposed a good while, which should seem that she is troubled with weighty causes."

July 7, 1574: Oxford and Elizabeth fight loudly enough to be overheard. Oxford storms out and travels to the Continent without permission—an act of treason by a high-ranking nobleman. Elizabeth continues on her summer progress.

July 28, 1574: Oxford is brought back by his friend
Thomas Bedingfield. He rejoins the progress at Bath.

September 1574: Anne, Oxford's Countess (now 18),
writes to Lord Sussex in his capacity as Lord
Chamberlain (not to be confused with Oxford's
hereditary title of Lord Great Chamberlain), to request
an additional room at Hampton Court for herself and
Edward during the coming visit. *"I shall think myself
greatly bound to you for it, for the more commodious
my lodging is the willinger I hope my Lord my
husband will be to come thither..."*

October 1574: Anne and Oxford spend October at
Hampton Court and have an "extra room" (Burghley's
diary).

January 1575: Oxford sets out for travels on the
Continent, this time with royal authorization. He
announces in open Court that if his wife, Anne, gives
birth it is not by him. He will be gone for 15 months.

March 1575: The Queen finds out that Anne is
pregnant. She appears pleased.

May 1575: Archbishop Matthew Parker dies.

July 2, 1575: Anne's daughter, Elizabeth Vere, is born.
(That puts conception in Sept/October. Oxford was still
in London.)

September 15, 1575: Oxford is touring throughout Italy.
He hears that his wife was delivered of a daughter,
Elizabeth, in July—He seems happy about it and
continues on his travels in Italy.

April 1576: Seven months later, Oxford, now in Paris, hears stories that, back in London, he is a laughing stock because of rumors that Elizabeth isn't his child. He returns to London in haste.

April 1576: Oxford separates from Anne for five years.

THE STORY

Elizabeth wants to make sure that, when the time comes, the child will be accepted as her dynastic heir. She consults with her trusted Archbishop of Canterbury, Matthew Parker, four times. The father, Edward de Vere, the 17th Earl of Oxford, accompanies her the first and the last time. Remembering Henry VIII and his bastard son, Henry Fitzroy, not to mention Queen Mary declaring herself legitimate, it doesn't seem that she actually needs to marry Oxford. However, secret marriages were common in Elizabethan England and she certainly could have done it if she had wanted to for the sake of respectability. The only people who have to know are Elizabeth, Oxford, Burghley and the Archbishop. However, in May 1575 the Archbishop dies leaving Burghley as the only person, besides the couple, who can testify from personal knowledge of a possible secret marriage.

It may be argued that, given the public nature of palace life, it would have been impossible to conceal a pregnancy. To refute that opinion it should be sufficient to remind ourselves of Elizabeth's many previous pregnancy rumors and to point out the bulkiness of contemporary women's clothing (those castles are cold). Also, at a future time, Elizabeth herself is kept in the dark about the pregnancy of Anne Vavasour, one of her own Ladies of the Bedchamber, until the day of the birth.

Sometime in May 1574 is the most logical time for the birth to have occurred. A short time later she and Oxford fight loudly and Oxford disappears to the Continent without permission. It also seems logical that the big fight had something to do with the baby because he apparently mentions it in the Sonnets (as spelled out by Hank Whittemore in *The Monument*). In Sonnet 33 Oxford records the "region cloud" (Elizabeth Regina) taking the baby away from him (probably to send him away with a wetnurse).

Sonnet 33:

Even so my sunne one early morn did shine,
With all triumphant splendor on my brow,
But out alack, he was but one hour mine,
The region cloud hath mask'd him from me now.

He comes back from his scandalously unauthorized visit to the Continent and, much to everyone's amazement, Elizabeth gives him a warm welcome, and then proceeds with him to Bath, where she is going for the curative, purifying waters.

Sonnet 154:

And so the General of hot desire,
Was sleeping by a Virgin hand disarmed.
This brand she quenched in a cool Well by,
Which from love's fire took heat perpetual,
Growing a bath and healthful remedy,
For men diseased, but I, my Mistress' thrall,
Came there for cure and this by that I prove,
Love's fire heats water, water cools not love.

It appears that the Queen and Oxford have made up and have come to some sort of agreement about their offspring.

Oxford's countess, Anne, now 18, is getting more mature and less willing to put up with her loveless marriage bed. The poor girl is reduced to begging for an additional room at Hampton Court where Oxford and the Queen, together, will plan his imminent European "Renaissance" tour. She's hoping that having an extra room will make it easier to get her husband alone and seduce him. It would appear that she succeeds because her child, Elizabeth Vere, is born nine months after their October stay with the "extra room" while Oxford is in Italy fulfilling his passion and his obligation as Minister of Culture.

Oxford, still traveling on his mission to discover the secrets of Renaissance Italy, seems pleased when he first learns of the baby and continues on his tour. Seven months later he hears rumors that Anne's child isn't his and that he is a laughing stock back in London. He believes the stories and races home, getting captured by pirates enroute and cast ashore naked (like Hamlet). On his return he spurns his wife and goes straight to the Queen. He stays away from Anne for five years.

CHAPTER 6

BUT HOW DO YOU HIDE A ROYAL CHILD? THE 2ND EARL OF SOUTHAMPTON

THE TIMELINE

June 1569: The disloyal 2nd Earl of Southampton (age 26) entertains Queen Elizabeth at his castle at Titchfield, Southampton, on the Southern coast of England.

June 1570: The 2nd Earl is arrested & confined incommunicado in the house of Beecher, a Sheriff of London, for activities involving the Catholic underground.

July 1570: He is transferred to the custody of William More, a family friend, at his country home in Loseley, near Guildford to be held until he proves his conformity by joining in the family prayers.

December 1570: Six months later, the Earl finally submits (joins in the More family's prayers) and is released.

October 1571: He is re-arrested for involvement in the Ridolfi plot to assassinate Elizabeth and put under "close imprisonment" (no visitors) in the Tower of London.

February 1572: The 2nd Earl continues to be held in the Tower under "close imprisonment." There are no charges and official English history does not explain it.

January 1573: The 2nd Earl's wife, the Countess of Southampton, age 20, becomes pregnant.

February 1573: The Countess writes to the Queen to plead for conjugal visits. The Queen turns her down.

February 14, 1573: The 2nd Earl writes a pleading letter to the privy council also begging for conjugal visits and mentioning the "previous heavy answer of her Majesty lately given to my poor wife …. After 16 months close imprisonment." The Privy Council turns him down.

May 1573: The 2nd Earl is released from the Tower after 18 months "close imprisonment" and he and his wife are placed at Cowdrey, his father-in-law's estate, once again under the supervision of William More.

October 6, 1573: The 2nd Earl writes to William More that his wife, the Countess, has given birth unexpectedly the night before to "A goodly boy" at Cowdrey, and apologizes for not being able to tell him in time to have Sir More's wife present, as was promised.

July 1574: The 2nd Earl of Southampton is placed on the commission of the Peace for Hampshire. He is also made a Commissioner for the transport of grain, a Commissioner of musters, and a Commissioner to suppress piracy.

April 1576: Thomas Dymock, a man of mystery, arrives at the 2nd Earl's home and takes over the household at the same time that a baby, Henry Wriothesley, the future 3rd Earl of Southampton, enters the household from 18 months of being wet-nursed. Dymock dominates the household, the 2nd Earl, his Countess and everything else.

January 1577: The 2nd Earl of Southampton forbids his wife to see "Donesame" any more. (He seems to believe his wife has been playing around again.)— Akrigg

January 1580: Early in the year he discovers that in spite of his warning, his wife has been seeing "Donesame" again and "banishes her from his board and presence" and sends her to go live at another estate he owns—Akrigg

March 1580: She writes to her father, Lord Montague, pleading for help because

"The life I have ledd these to (two) yeares, with the bitterness which I have with patience endured, hath byn sufficient to satisfy for so muche as I ever erred in, but by many other accidents I well fynde it is not my falt but myself he hateth for my frendes sake, whom long he hath mislyked with small reason, truly, if he remember the tyme past."

She's been banished from her husband's home and from the child for the last 2 years and been kept under close watch. Her husband is dealing with her only through Dymock, whom she hates. *"...this howse is not for them that will not honor Dymocke as a god."*

January 1581: The 2nd Earl is once more imprisoned because of new anti-Catholic laws.

June 24,1581: He is released. He is only 35 years old but he makes out his will and appoints Thomas Dymock as executor of his estate.

August 1581: The 2nd Earl is arrested again after being set up by Dymoke so that the crown finds out he has been in touch with Edmund Campion, the Catholic traitor.

September 1581: A month later he is released & returns to Tichfield.

October 4,1581: A short time after that the 2nd Earl of Southampton dies at age 35 under the watchful eye of Thomas Dymock, at Tichfield. In his will he disowns his own daughter if she ever lives with her mother.

November 1581: The Countess of Southampton reports that she hasn't seen her "lyttle sonne" for almost 2 years.

December 1581: The 2nd Earl's official son, the 3rd Earl of Southampton (Henry Wriothesley, age 7), enters Burghley House as a royal ward of the Queen.

THE STORY

The 2nd Earl of Southampton, a devout Catholic, gets more and more involved with subversive, anti-Elizabeth Catholics and, as a result, is repeatedly in trouble with the Queen's government. It gets to the point that he is put away in the Tower of London for participating in the Ridolphi plot to kill the queen and put Mary, Queen of Scots on the throne. Then something odd happens. He isn't charged or sentenced, but he is kept in "close imprisonment" in the Tower. No visitors! No official mention is made, but the Crown seems to have some special interest in holding him incommunicado. I believe it's highly likely that the crown's interest centers around his wife, the Countess of Southampton, who seems to have acquired a boyfriend during her husband's imprisonment. She has conceived and carries a child, which her husband doesn't know about and, because he has been under "close imprisonment" in the Tower for 14 months, can't possibly be his. Like any guilty wife would, she tries to camouflage her infidelity by getting permission from the Queen for conjugal visits. The Queen turns her down. In desperation, she then gets her husband to beg the Privy Council for conjugal visits, and they turn him down, too. No one seems to want to help the Countess fool her husband.

It's time for the Crown to make him an offer he can't refuse: They inform him of his wife's infidelity and offer him freedom plus other remuneration, in exchange for not making a public fuss over her bastard child. On May 1st, 1573 he is released from the Tower. He is allowed to live with his pregnant wife at his in-laws house under the supervision of William More who lives at Lowsley, a short distance away. Five months later, on October 6th, he notifies his ex-jailer that his wife has suddenly given birth during the night to a "goodly boy" and apologizes for not being able to notify Sir More's wife in time for her to be present at the birth, as he evidently had promised to do.

It appears that the Crown has been keeping close tabs on the Countess' pregnancy and has even arranged for a trusted female representative to be present at the birth, although, in the event, she is unable to do so. The 2nd Earl is doing his reportorial duty by informing Sir More of the birth of "a goodly boy" to his wife but doesn't seem to take much paternal pleasure in the fact that this is his first son and heir. On the other hand, he will have other things to be pleased with. The Crown appoints him to the Commission on Peace, the Commission on Grain transport and the Commissions of Musters and Piracy suppression, all of which have stipends. His wife is probably trying to be extra nice to him to make amends for her infidelity, and the baby is off being wet-nursed. All things considered, life is not too bad.

Two years pass and it's time to bring the baby home from being wet-nursed. I know that sounds absurd to twenty-first century sensibilities, but in the pre-formula 16th Century it was a mark of social standing for aristocratic women to farm out their children to wet-nurses for 18 to 36 months. It was also favored by husbands because of the widespread belief that nursing women should refrain from sex. They believed it affected the milk. The nurses frequently lived away from population centers from fear of the plague, which meant that the parents had limited contact. Also, in those days, a baby's survival was so precarious that it made practical sense not to become too attached until the infant had a good grip on life.

It's at this point that I believe a baby-switch probably took place (a "changling child" according to Oberon). The Earl's "Goodly Boy" is born on October 6th, 1573. If he is nursed for about 24 to 36 months and if Elizabeth's "changling child" is born in May of 1574 and is nursed for 18 to 30 months, it could work out—they could easily be switched. Just before the baby comes home, a man named Thomas Dymock arrives at Titchfield. It's unknown how he gets there, but he immediately takes charge of the 2nd Earl's household. Dymock seems to be in charge of everything involving the baby boy and insists on doing everything his own way, much to the consternation of the Countess who complains bitterly to her father about Dymock and how her husband lets him run the household.

Thomas Dymock is a mystery character in this story and very little is known about him. Possibly, he's a son of the Queen's official Ceremonial Champion, Sir Edward Dymock. He would have to be totally trustworthy. In any case, he seems to be the crown's representative in the 2nd Earl's home. He rules the Southampton household from the time he arrives, simultaneously with the baby, for the next five and one half years until the 2nd Earl dies and the baby (Henry Wriothesley, 3rd Earl of Southampton and now a boy of seven) is sent to live with Lord Burghley as a ward of the Queen. The 2nd Earl even makes Dymock the executor of his will and also a beneficiary. In the will, Dymock is designated to have total control over the child and is also given life-rights to live in one of the 2nd Earl's estates. He shows up again in the history books twenty years later, in 1594, still living on Southampton's estate and helping him hide the murderous Danvers brothers from the law.

One may legitimately wonder why the 2nd Earl would agree to bring up a royal child as one of his own and, given that he was a treasonous Catholic, how could he be trusted? In the first place, he probably didn't know for sure whose baby it was—only that the Crown wanted it brought up as his son. Plus, there were several compelling reasons for him to co-operate. As a Catholic recusant with a reputation for involvement in plots against the Queen, he was constantly risking arrest. England was a police state and the Crown could sweep him up and execute him on a whim. The threat of death (and I'm sure they threatened) is a very persuasive argument. As it turns out, by agreeing to the baby switch, he bought himself seven years of life and freedom during which it is reported he spent money like a drunken sailor.

("We find him impoverishing himself, lavishing funds upon the building of his great new mansion at Dogmersfield and maintaining a retinue much larger than he needed. After his years of deprivation in the tower the Earl was in a mood to deny himself nothing."—Akrigg)

From the crown's point of view, a treasonous Catholic household would be the last place anyone would look for a hidden prince.

Fig. 4 - Mary Browne, wife of
the 2nd Earl of Southampton.

He also gets even with his wife who has cheated on him. It makes no difference to him which baby he takes home—neither one is his. In fact, he would probably rather take the crown's changling child over his wife's bastard. He hates his wife for her unfaithfulness, which is documented in his will where he disowns his daughter if she ever lives with her mother. And lastly, instead of being attainted, his family name of Southampton will live on in honor. Not a bad bargain.

After seven years of freedom he is back in prison for two brief visits. After the first he makes out his will (premonition or knowledge?). One month after his second release he dies, at the tender age of 35. He is probably poisoned – slowly. The timing is most likely determined by the fact that the changling child has officially reached the Age of Reason as defined by the Church (age seven) and is no longer considered a child. It's time to start his education to become a Prince, which means getting him to London.

Since the Countess complains so bitterly about Dymock and the household arrangements, she doesn't seem to be "in on it." I don't think she realizes that the baby who is returned from the wet-nurse is not hers. So, what became of her baby, the "goodly boy?" No one knows, but, in his will, the 2nd Earl leaves a curious bequest for the education, to the age of 21, of "William my beggars boye."

CHAPTER 7

OXFORD'S BACHELOR YEARS
1576 – 1581

THE TIMELINE

April 1576: Separated from his wife, the 17th Earl of Oxford lives like a bachelor on Broad Street, not far from the Theatre Inns on Bishopsgate and near Burbage's revolutionary new structure, the very first building in London designed specifically to put on plays, aptly named THE THEATRE.

April 1576: Oxford writes a letter to his father-in-law, Lord Burghley, saying he wants nothing to do with Burghley's daughter and not to bring her anywhere near him. He even gets the Queen to bar Anne from Court when he's around (she's a Lady in Waiting) so he won't have to see her.

June 1576: A book of poetry is published: The PARADYSE OF DAYNTYE DEVISES contains seven poems signed E.O.

January 1577: THE HISTORIE OF ERROR (anonymous) is performed at Court by St. Paul's Boys on New Year's Day at night. (Early version of COMEDY OF ERRORS—Eva Turner Clark)

1577: Holinshed publishes his CHRONICLES on which many of Shakespeare's history plays are based.

February 1577: THE HISTORIE OF THE SOLITARIE KNIGHT (anonymous) is played at Whitehall Palace by The Chamberlain's Men (Early version of TIMON OF ATHENS—Eva Turner Clark).

February 1577: THE HISTORYE OF TITUS AND GISIPPUS (anonymous) is performed at Whitehall by St Paul's Boys (probably an early version of TITUS ANDRONICUS – Eva Turner Clark).

December 1577: "I hear he is about to buy a house here in London about Watling Street, and not to continue a Courtier as he hath done." - Duchess of Suffolk writing to Burghley about Oxford.

December 1577: Peregrine Bertie marries Mary Vere (Oxford's half sister) against everyone's advice because she is reputed to have an "evil tongue like her brother." Six years later the Queen will send Peregrine to Denmark as an ambassador. Things he observes in Denmark are recorded in HAMLET.

January 1578: Oxford starts an affair with Anne Vavasour, a Lady of the Queen's bedchamber.

January 1578: THE RAPE OF THE SECOND HELEN (anonymous) is performed at court. (An early version of ALL'S WELL THAT ENDS WELL - Eva Turner Clark).

September 1578: Frobisher's 3rd voyage to find gold returns with a hold full of worthless ore. Oxford is a major investor and loses it all. Oxford accuses Michael

48

Lock of swindling him. The court agrees. Michael Lock goes to the Fleet Prison and "Shylock" is born.

December 1578: AN HISTORY OF THE CRUELTIES OF A STEPMOTHER (anonymous) is performed by The Lord Chamberlains Men at Richmond Court (early version of CYMBELINE—Eva Turner Clark).

January 1579: A MORRAL OF THE MARRYAGE OF MYNDE AND MEASURE (anonymous), performed at Court by St Paul's Boys. (Thought by some to be about the marriage of Oxford's sister (she of the evil tongue) to Peregrine Bertie. Early version of THE TAMING OF THE SHREW—Eva Turner Clark).

Jan 1579: THE HISTORY OF THE RAPE OF THE SECOND HELEN (anonymous) is performed by the Chamberlain's Men at Richmond Court (an early version of ALL'S WELL THAT ENDS WELL—Eva Turner Clark.).

February 1579: THE HISTORY OF PORTIO AND DEMORANTES (anonymous) was shown at Whitehall on Candlemas day at night by The Lord Chamberlains men (early MERCHANT OF VENICE—Eva Turner Clark).

March 1579: The Chamberlain's Men at court perform THE HISTORY OF MURDEROUS MICHAEL by Oxford (early version of ARDEN OF FEVERSHAM which is early version of 2 HENRY VI—Eva Turner Clark).

July 1579: THE JEW (anonymous) performed at The Bull (another early version of THE MERCHANT OF VENICE—Eva Turner Clark).

December 1579: Chamberlain's Men at court perform A HISTORY OF THE DUKE OF MILAN AND THE MARQUIS OF MANTUA (early version of TWO GENTLEMEN OF VERONA—Eva Turner Clark).

1580-85: Oxford sells extensive properties.

January 1580: Oxford buys Fisher's Folly which is where Devonshire Square is now. It's an expensive mansion and he does extensive renovations to it. He transforms it into a sort of writing academy and workshop. In 1881 an historian described a still-standing section of the original building: ***"It was of the Elizabethan age, and one room contained a rich cornice of masks, fruit, and leaves, connected by ribands** (ribbons**). In another there were, over the fireplace, the arms of Henry Wriothesley, Earl of Southampton . . . Shakespeare's friend."*** (*Old and New London – The City Ancient and Modern* by Walter Thornbury, 1881, p. 158).

January 1580: Oxford organizes OXFORD'S MEN out of the Earl of Warwick's men and they go out on the road to Dover, Norwich, Coventry and Bristol.

January 1580: Oxford converts space in Blackfriars Convent into a public theater featuring choir-boy players.

December 1580: Oxford & Lord Henry Howard have a public falling-out. Oxford confesses in front of the Queen and French ambassador that he has taken part in treasonous Catholic meetings with Lord Howard, Charles Arundel & Francis Southwell. According to the official record, Oxford is placed in the Tower of London along with the others.

January 1, 1581: Twelve days later, Oxford gives Queen Elizabeth a jeweled unicorn as a New Year's Day gift.

January 1581: A few days after that, a huge royal Jousting Tournament is held. Oxford is triumphant and resplendent as the "Knight of the Tree of the Sun."

March 23, 1581: Two months after that, Anne Vavasour gives birth to Oxford's illegitimate son, Edward Vere. In a jealous fury, the Queen throws them both in the Tower.

June 1581: After two and a half months, Oxford is released from the Tower, but the Queen puts him under house arrest (Ogburn, *The Man Who Was Shakespeare* (1995), p. 53) and banishes him from Court.

THE STORY

After Oxford leaves his wife, he goes through a period of getting the bad taste out of his mouth. In his mind, she has disgraced him and the noble name of Oxford. In a 1576 collection of poems (PARADYSE OF DAYNTYE DEVISES) there are seven poems signed E.O. (Edward Oxenford) on themes of disgrace and loss of good name:

Loss of Good Name.

Fram'd in the front of forlorn hope past all recovery,
I stayless stand, to abide the shock of shame and infamy.

51

My life, through ling'ring long, is lodg'd in lair of loathsome
ways;
My death delay'd to keep from life the harm of hapless days.
My sprites, my heart, my wit and force, in deep distress are
drown'd;
The only loss of my good name is of these griefs the ground.

Then he immerses himself in writing plays and begins to churn out scripts for Paul's Boys, The Children of the Chapel and The Lord Chamberlain's Men to perform for the entertainment of Elizabeth and her court. They are all anonymous but seem to be early versions of plays we all know under different names which history has credited to Shakespeare. Being a perfectionist and a born showman he probably feels the need to improve some of the talent and arranges for Paul's Boys to also give performances for the public. This gives the boys more 'stage time' to polish for Court performances. It's also a chance to test his writing skills with a more diverse audience. He converts a space in the old Blackfriars nunnery, near St Paul's, for this purpose.

He sets to work carrying out his responsibilities as Minister of Culture, putting his own money into it. He's investing in the Tudor Dynasty, his son's dynasty and therefore—his dynasty! He buys Fisher's Folly mansion and renovates it (lavishly) into a writing workshop to nourish and support talented young men he thinks can help create an English writing culture in what is still a mostly illiterate country. John Lyly, Thomas Watson, Anthony Mundy along with Robert Greene and Thomas Nashe are among the group. Over the fireplace he mounts the arms of the 3rd Earl of Southampton (now age eight) as a reminder of what all of this is for.

He seems determined to create a literate Renaissance in England and make it into a cultural center, like Italy. He even wears Italian clothes in spite of the fact that he is ridiculed for being "A mirror of Tuscanismo."

He writes play after play (at least seven are performed in 1579). As an aristocrat, it is socially forbidden for him to be known as a playwright, so most of the plays are anonymous.

It's an amazing period of creativity for Oxford and he works hard. He also begins an affair with Anne Vavasour, a dark-haired beauty who is one of the Queen's Maids of Honor. Between the Queen's well-known jealousy and Anne's feisty relatives, the Knyvets, it's a risky romance.

Somewhere along the way he figures out that he has been deceived; not by his wife, but by vicious slanders invented by Henry Howard, aided and abetted by Charles Arundel. He discovers that the rumor of Anne Cecil cheating on him with another man had been started by Lord Howard in order to cause a rift between himself and Anne's father, Lord Burghley. These lies have caused him public shame and humiliation, not to mention ruining his personal life. Oxford is related to the Howard family and even has a literary connection, since Henry Howard's father, the Earl of Surrey (also named Henry Howard) wrote the first poems in the form that would eventually be adopted by Oxford and is referred to today as the "Shakespearean" form. Unfortunately, his son is skilled mostly in the art of intrigue. As a devout Catholic, he continually plots to remove Elizabeth from the throne and replace her with Mary, Queen of Scots. From his perspective, Oxford's crime is that he married the daughter of Lord Burghley, protector of Protestantism, after he and the Queen had executed Henry's brother (Thomas Howard, 4th Duke of Norfolk) for his part in the Ridolphi plot. If Henry can split them apart it will be a serious crack in Elizabeth's court and revenge for the execution of his brother. This is a personal, as well as religious, war.

I'm convinced that Henry Howard is Oxford's real life Iago who plants the rumors about Anne and her baby to make this happen. His negative PR succeeds so well that Oxford leaves his wife and spends the next five years ignoring her while writing, building theatres, developing

Fig. 5 - The infamous Tower of London,
where Oxford spent several months in 1581.

theatre companies and impregnating his mistress. Eventually though, he finds out the truth and gets his revenge. He would later say, "The Howards were the most treacherous race under Heaven" and "my Lord Howard was the worst villain that lived in this earth."

Catholicism is popular among the nobility. No one talks about it but Elizabeth has many Catholic friends and relatives, including Henry Howard. She can't believe they'll plot against her. I suspect that Oxford is helping Burghley to make the Queen face up to the reality of the Catholic danger among her nobles. Also, possibly, Oxford wants to make amends to Burghley for being so wrong about his daughter all these years.

On December 20, 1580, they stage a showdown in front of the Queen with the French Ambassador on hand as a warning to the French. Oxford gets down on his knees before the Queen and confesses that he has been in secret, treasonous, Catholic meetings with Henry Howard, Charles Arundel and Francis Southwell. In retaliation, they make dreadful allegations against Oxford which make it into the record. The official record says they are all put in the Tower but there is no evidence of Oxford actually being incarcerated so we are forced to conclude that he must have been functioning as an undercover agent for Burghley in order to trap the others. This is supported by the fact that only twelve days later, on New Years Day, Oxford gives Elizabeth a golden pin in the shape of a unicorn studded with jewels, symbolizing a wild mythic creature surrendering himself to pure love. Three weeks after that, Oxford takes part in a huge royal jousting tournament and wins as "The Knight of the Tree of the Sun." Far from being in disgrace, it appears that Oxford is in high favor with the crown.

CHAPTER 8

HENRY WRIOTHESLEY, 3RD EARL OF SOUTHAMPTON - THE BOY

THE TIMELINE

April 1581: A group of French ambassadors arrives in London to negotiate a marriage between Elizabeth and Hercule Francois duc d'Alençon, (youngest son of Henri II of France), and are royally entertained with the first performance of A MIDSUMMER NIGHT'S DREAM. (Eva Turner Clark).

December 1581: Henry Wriothesley, 3rd Earl of Southampton (age seven), enters Cecil House as a royal ward where he probably meets and bonds with 16-year-old Robert Devereux, Earl of Essex, who is also a ward. He also meets Robert Cecil, Burghley's hunchbacked son, who is 18.

October 1585: Henry enters St John's College at Cambridge (age eleven and a half).

March 1588: He is admitted to Gray's Inn for legal study.

June 1589: He receives the degree of Master of Arts from Cambridge after being in residence for four years.

THE STORY

Queen Elizabeth uses her beauty, her fame and her unmarried state to tease many foreign Royals into believing she is looking for a husband and in so doing solves many diplomatic crises and maintains peace for England. Her most serious-looking romance is with Alençon, the youngest son of Henri II of France. Young, pockmarked and ugly, he evidently still makes a deep impression on Elizabeth, who has kept him on a string for several years. The English people nickname him "Monsieur" and are massively against the match. In 1581 many people, including her old boyfriend, Dudley (Lord Leicester), think she might actually marry him. Eight French ambassadors, among whom is La Mothe Fenelon, arrive to firm up the deal. Imagine her surprise and embarrassment when the entertainment she has ordered for their amusement, written by her favorite court writer, Edward de Vere, the 17th Earl of Oxford, (recently put in the Tower for fathering Anne Vavasour's baby) turns out to be a very funny play containing a satire on the Queen and Alençon and her current predicament regarding an heir.

In the play, Bottom, the weaver, is put under a spell, given a jackass head and speaks bad French, constantly mispronouncing the word "monsieur." Titania, Queen of the Fairies (Elizabeth), is also put under a spell and falls in love with him. She lavishes her affections on the jackass/man and commands her fairies to care for him. Her fairies are named: Peaseblossom, Cobweb, Mustardseed and Moth (similar to La Mothe).

PUCK: *The King doth keep his revels here tonight;*
Take heed the Queen come not within his sight;
For Oberon is passing fell and wrath,

Because that she as her attendant hath
A lovely boy stolen from an Indian king;
She never had so sweet a changeling.
And jealous Oberon would have the child
Knight of his train, to trace the forests wild;
But she, perforce, withholds the loved boy

Oxford, as Oberon, is reminding the Queen that there is no reason to marry that ugly jackass of a Frenchman in order to produce an heir since their own secret prince is now old enough to be moved to London so that Oxford can take charge of his education for the throne. (Thank God, the French won't get the joke). It was probably part of their bargain struck at Bath that, until the boy reaches the age of reason (seven), he (Oxford) won't try to contact him or even know what his name is. That time has now arrived and Oxford and Burghley are in agreement—it's time to bring the boy to London. But Elizabeth is probably terrified of having him in London in such close proximity to her. A secret baby 80 miles away in Titchfield (three to four days by carriage) is one thing. Having a seven year old son living right at Court is quite another. God forbid someone should notice a resemblance. (The boy has red hair and blue eyes just like hers. So does Oxford!).

OBERON: *Why should Titania cross her Oberon?*
I do but beg a little changeling boy,
To be my henchman.

TITANIA: *Set your heart at rest;*
The fairy land buys not the child of me.

Apparently she changes her mind, because eight months later the seven-year-old Southampton arrives at Cecil house to live with Baron Burghley as a Royal ward. (In Act IV we abruptly learn that Titania has, in fact, turned over the boy to Oberon. But that may not have been in the version the Queen saw.) At the same time, Oxford reunites with his wife Anne, which means he can visit his father-in-law whenever he wants and watch over the boy and be a "secret father" to him. He can supervise his education without the boy, or anyone else, knowing the real relationship. I'm tantalized by the possibility that Southampton becomes a choirboy with the Children of the Chapel, allowing Oxford to give him a lot of personal attention and also to give the Queen a chance to see him at services, when they sing, and also when they perform plays at court, without arousing any suspicion.

The Cecil wardship academy kicks in and gives him a superb education followed by college where he becomes a real scholar, spending a full four years at Cambridge (unusual for an aristocrat) and receives a Masters Degree.

CHAPTER 9

OXFORD - THE BANISHMENT YEARS 1581—1583

THE TIMELINE

March 1581: Oxford is put in the Tower because of the birth of his son Edward Vere by Anne Vavasour who is one of Elizabeth's Ladies of the Bedchamber. (He remains there until June 8—then under house arrest (Ogburn, *The Man Who Was Shakespeare* (1995), p. 53) for the rest of the year before being banished from court.

July 1581: Thomas Knyvet, the uncle of Anne Vavasour, kills one of Oxford's men in a street brawl (as Tybalt kills Mercutio in ROMEO & JULIET).

September 1581: ROMEO & JULIET, date of original composition: *"'Tis since the earthquake now eleven years"* (Act I, Scene 3) refers to the famous earthquake of 1570, centered near Verona in Ferrara, which produced over 2000 aftershocks over three months— Eva Turner Clark).

March 1582: Thomas Knyvet and Oxford duel. Both are hurt but Oxford gets the worst of it. He is lame for the rest of his life.

January 1583: Burghley reports that Oxford "is ruined and in adversity" and has only four servants.

February 1583: A HISTORIE OF ARIODANTE AND GENEUORA (anonymous) played at court. (Probably an early version of MUCH ADO ABOUT NOTHING. Since Oxford was banished it was performed by Mr Mulcaster's Children—Eva Turner Clark.)

May 1583: A son is born to Oxford and Anne Cecil. He dies in infancy

THE STORY

In a world without contraception or safe abortions it's not surprising that eventually Anne Vavasour gives birth to Oxford's child. The Queen doesn't find out until the day of his birth. She's furious and puts them both in the tower. Two and a half months later he is out under house arrest, and the Queen continues to banish him from court. She's so upset with him that the banishment lasts for two years. She won't even let Oxford's children's companies perform at court.

It would appear that, with Anne Vavasour and the murder of one of his men fresh in mind, he writes ROMEO AND JULIET, but little else is known of Oxford's life during these years except that he and Anne have a boy who dies in infancy and is buried at Castle Hedingham, Oxford's ancestral home. Probably, he spends a lot of time teaching and training young Henry.

CHAPTER 10

THE CONNECTION - SOUTHAMPTON, ESSEX & ROBERT CECIL

THE TIMELINE

December 1581: Henry Wriothesley, The 3rd Earl of Southampton, age eight (actually only seven) enters Burghley House as the 8th and last royal ward of Queen Elizabeth's reign.

1584: Robert Cecil, at 21, travels abroad to Europe and France carrying with him a list of "precepts" from his father (like Polonius gives to Laertes in HAMLET).

1585: Essex (20), with the help of the Earl of Leicester, his step-father and long-time "favorite" of the Queen, is granted early release from wardship and enters Parliament.

1585: Essex sails to the Low Countries with Leicester, who has taken him under his wing. It's the start of his apprenticeship as a soldier and as the next "Queen's favorite."

October 1585: Southampton enters St John's College at Cambridge (age eleven and a half) and stays for four years.

1584 & 1586: Robert Cecil sits Parliament for Westminster

1587: Elizabeth appoints Essex as her Master of the Horse, replacing Leicester, who is ailing. Essex is now known as her "favorite."

March 1588: Leicester, not in good health, is put in charge of the land army in preparation for the Spanish invasion.

April 1588: Essex is made Knight of the Garter

June 1588: Anne Cecil dies (age 31) in the Royal Palace of Greenwich (rumored a suicide like Ophelia) and is buried in Westminster Abbey. Many women, but few men, attend (war preparations?). Oxford & Queen are not there.

September 1588: Robert, Earl of Leicester ("Robin") dies of illness. The Queen is devastated.

October 1588: The Spanish Armada is defeated by bad weather and good English sailing. Oxford is in his own ship but it gets crippled in a sea battle. The English have gained enormous pride but the war with Spain drags on until 1603

December 1588: The Queen's first Christmas without Leicester. She shows great favor to Essex

1589: Cecil sits Parliament for Hertfordshire.

April 1589: Essex, looking for action and good press sneaks out behind Elizabeth's back and goes marauding with Francis Drake, raiding the coasts of Spain and Portugal like pirates.

July 1589: Essex's agents make secret overtures to James VI of Scotland as Elizabeth's most logical successor.

1591: Robert Cecil wins a seat on the Privy Council

1593: Essex wins a seat on the Privy Council

1596: Robert Cecil is appointed Secretary of State

THE STORY

When seven-year old Henry Wriothsley steps into Burghley House there are no other wards in residence. Robert Devereux, (16), the 2nd Earl of Essex, is a ward but is no longer a full-time resident in Burghley House. He has five more years to run on his wardship and one more year to go before graduating from Trinity College at Cambridge, so he is a sometime presence. More frequently around is Robert Cecil, Burghley's son, still at St. John's College at Cambridge. These two teenage boys, both named Robert, pursuing their own ambitions, will frame the course of Henry's life from here on.

Robert Devereux is a dynamic young aristocrat, a man of action who cuts a handsome and dramatic figure. His ambition is to get political power by the customary aristocratic route: becoming a military hero. He is encouraged by his step-father, the Earl of Leicester, Lord Dudley, the Queen's now old "favorite" who will take young Essex under his wing and groom him to replace himself not only as Commander of the Armies but also as

Elizabeth's "favorite." Young Southampton probably idolizes Essex and looks up to him as a heroic model. He will become a close friend and follower and will even marry Essex's cousin, Elizabeth Vernon, in preference to Burghley's granddaughter. Essex and many other lords come to believe that the Cecils are leading England and the aristocracy toward a future subservient to Spain. He makes secret contacts with James VI of Scotland because James seems to be the logical candidate to follow heirless Elizabeth and he's hoping that he (Essex) can become the power behind the throne instead of Robert Cecil. Under his stepfather's guidance, he will make his name as a swashbuckler on the battlefield, and is already something of a star figure. By the late 1580's he has been appointed the Queen's Master of the Horse, been made a Knight of the Garter and is being referred to as the Queen's "favorite."

God only knows what the boy thinks of Robert Cecil. In the 16th Century most people believed that your physical appearance was a sign from God of your true nature. A dwarfish, hunchback dressed in black robes would always be suspected of being as deformed on the inside as he is on the outside. To seven-year old Henry Wriothesley he must have been more than a little bit scary. But, scary or not, Burghley is grooming his second son to become a statesman and fill his shoes when the time comes. In preparation, Robert gets himself elected to Parliament several times from several different districts.

While Essex is becoming a military star and Cecil is climbing the ladder of bureaucratic success, Southampton is being trained for kingship by his father, Oxford, who conceals his real relationship. He watches over his son from his vantage point of running the children's acting companies and also by being Burghley's recently returned prodigal son-in-law and therefore an unremarked visitor at Burghley House.

The Cecil wardship academy kicks in and gives young Southampton a superb education followed by college where he becomes a real scholar, spending a full four years at Cambridge (unusual for an aristocrat) and receives a Masters Degree.

Over the years a serious competition grows between Essex and Robert Cecil as to which man will have the Queen's ear. The competition is real but Elizabeth may encourage it because it suits her purposes of keeping everyone a little off-balance.

CHAPTER 11

OXFORD IS RESTORED TO FAVOR

THE TIMELINE

June 1583: The Queen finally restores Oxford to favor. Burghley has to recruit Raleigh to help convince her (She's still mad at Oxford): "whilst we seek for favour [for Oxford], all crosses are laid against him, and by untruths sought to be kept in disgrace. And he punished as far or farther than any like crime hath been, first by her Majesty, and then by the drab's (Anne Vavasour's) friend (Thomas Knyvet) in revenge to the peril of his life."

June 1583: Spymaster Walsingham, who is a Puritan, instructs Master of the Revels, Tilney, to form an acting company to be called The Queen's Men. The core company will be twelve of the best actors in London and is to be, primarily, a touring company, without a permanent home in London. (***The Queen's Men were formed to spread Protestant and royalist propaganda through a divided realm and to close a breach within radical Protestantism.***"—*The Queen's Men and Their Plays*—Scott McMillin & Sally-Beth MacLean)

June 1583: At the same time, Oxford forms London's largest children's company, Oxford's Boys, by joining The Children of the Chapel & The Children of St Paul's into one company. He acquires a lease on Blackfriars Theatre & transfers it to his secretary, John Lyly

1583-1585: For the two seasons of 1583-84 and 1584-85 all court performances are by either Oxford's Boys or the Queen's Men. *No other companies perform at court.*

December 26, 1583: The Queen's Men present an unknown play for the Queen at Whitehall before taking it on the road.

December 29, 1583: The Queen's Men preview FIVE PLAYS IN ONE (by Tarlton) for the Queen at Whitehall.

January 1584: Oxford lends his secretary, Lyly, to the Queens Men.

March 1584: SAPHO AND PHAO by Lyly given at Court by Oxford's Boys. (Same subject as TWELFTH NIGHT.)

March 1584: Queen's Men preview ANTIC PLAY & COMEDY (anonymous) for the Queen at Court on Shrove Tuesday.

June 1584: Oxford is working at his studio, Fisher's Folly.

October 1584: Treachery seems to be everywhere, so Burghley & Privy Council create the "Bond of Association" to guarantee loyalty by swearing everyone to an oath to avenge any threat to Elizabeth.

December 1584: The Queen's Men preview PHYLLIDA & CORIN (anonymous) for the Queen at

Greenwich. (an early version of MIDSUMMER NIGHT'S DREAM—Eva Turner Clark.)

December 1584: AGAMEMMNON AND ULYSSES by John Lyly performed at court by Oxford's Boys. (An early version of TROILUS & CRESSIDA—Eva Turner Clark.)

January 1585: The Queen's Men preview FELIX & PHILOMENA for the Queen. (An early version of TWO GENTLEMEN OF VERONA—Eva Turner Clark.)

June 1586: An extraordinary annuity of £1,000/yr (Current value: £218,900/$313,979) is granted to Oxford by the Queen retroactive to March with no accounting to be required by the Exchequer. The money comes from Walsingham's spy budget. This annuity continues for the rest of his life.

THE STORY

1583 is a watershed year for Oxford. In June he is finally restored to the Queen's favor. As part of his return to favor she puts him to work doing what he loves best—theatre. But now there is to be a larger, patriotic purpose.

For years it has been obvious that, sooner or later, the Spanish will invade England. The only question is when. What will they find when they come ashore?—a populace fragmented and vulnerable because of religious and regional difference or unified behind their Tudor Queen against the foreign invaders? What is needed is a major propaganda campaign to educate the English people on the glories of being English and the virtues of the Tudor Dynasty in preserving civil peace in England for the last one hundred years. What they create is the forerunner of our US Office of War Information (OWI) during World War II, except that, instead of recruiting Frank Capra and using the movies, the Queen recruits Lord Oxford and uses the most popular art form of that day, the theatre. It would appear that Oxford is put in charge of the artistic side of this ambitious undertaking for obvious reasons—he's the only person with the theatre skills and the only one the Queen trusts to do the work and keep his identity hidden so the plays won't be recognized as government propaganda. He also has the best possible personal motive to do an exceptional job: He will be using his unique, special talents to make sure there is an England for his son to reign over after the invasion. Not just an England but a great and cultured England. He has the Queen's complete trust, and it seems that his functions as Minister of Culture have expanded to include Propaganda. Again, accountable directly to the Queen.

As part of this effort, the Master of the Revels, Tilney, on the orders of spymaster Walsingham, a Puritan with personal, religious objections to theatre, founds a new theatrical company specifically designed to tour the countryside —The Queen's Men. Tilney is the front man but Oxford is in artistic charge. Traveling players have always been used by the government to carry messages and keep their eyes and ears open in the taverns and on the streets wherever they go. However, the Queen's Men has a more focused political purpose. It's an elite company formed around twelve of the best actors in London whose major function is to go out into the hinterlands of England and, not only keep their eyes and ears open, but also perform plays written expressly to make unified, loyal citizens out the polyglot population of England, teach them the glory of being English and prepare them for the inevitable invasion from Catholic Spain. In Spring, Summer and Fall the actors have a grueling schedule frequently involving dividing themselves into two companies in order to perform in more towns. However, since they are stars, they are paid double the going rate for this valuable service (as noted in *The Queen's Men and Their Plays* (1998), p. 44) and, in Winter, they return to London and learn the new repertory for the following season. They have no theatre of their own in London, but from November to March they rehearse and preview the new plays for the Queen. They also play irregularly for the public as part of their rehearsal process and also because Londoners need to be influenced too. In the seasons of 1583-84 and 1584-85 no other adult company performs for the Queen. Oxford soon lends his secretary, John Lyly, to manage the company while he gets busy writing, and supervising others to write plays for the company to perform. He's running a sort of writing studio/factory at Fisher's Folly.

This pattern of rehearsing and previewing plays for the Queen's approval in the winter and then going out on the road in the warmer months continues until the Spanish Armada is defeated in 1588. It includes performances of the anonymous plays THE FAMOUS VICTORIES OF HENRY V (an early version of HENRY IV and HENRY V) and THE TROUBLESOME REIGN OF KING JOHN (an early version of KING JOHN) in the winter of 1586-87. In December of 1591, the Queen's Men give their last performance for the Queen, although they continue on as a company.

As if he didn't have enough to do, Oxford has joined the Children of the Chapel and St Paul's Boys into one company called Oxford's Boys and is busy writing plays for them to perform at Court. He even converts a space in the Blackfriars monastery into an indoor theatre and lets them perform for the public. Now the company can do more ambitious plays and do them better because of the larger talent pool (which helps casting) and the increased stage time for the boys (which improves their skills). In the seasons of 1583-84 and 1584-85 Oxford's Boys is the *only* children's company to perform at court. Between the Queen's Men and Oxford's Boys, Lord Oxford has a total monopoly on court performances and thus seems to have acquired an unheard-of importance in the eyes of Queen Elizabeth.

The plays done by the boys at court frequently contain satires on known court members who are probably in attendance, giving them the flavor of a Friars' Club Roast which is why modern day audiences don't always "get" the humor. Too many 'inside' jokes. Oxford is publically silent but his plays are outspoken and frequently skewer his fellow courtiers, earning him considerable enmity. He has a weapon no one else has—the ability to humiliate people in front of the Queen and the whole court and get away with it—as long as the Queen laughs.

Theatre is an expensive hobby and all this theatrical activity on behalf of the crown is costing Oxford much more than he can afford. He has always thought of it as equivalent to the money it costs a noble to go to war for his Queen. But show business is more expensive than war and, being something of a spendthrift anyway, he's already sold off most of his inherited property. His investments (notably the failed Frobisher voyage) have come to naught, the Queen hasn't come through with any of her promised largess and his income has been severely reduced. After lengthy petitions, the Queen finally grants him a £1,000/yr annuity, with no accounting to be required by the Exchequer. It is paid out of Walsingham's black box spy account. It's a lot, but not enough, and it comes with baggage:

> Dromio: *"I buy a thousand pound a year! I buy a rope."*
> (*Comedy of Errors*, Act IV, Sc 1)

I suspect that "the rope" is Elizabeth's way of keeping him in his place.

CHAPTER 12

HAPPY BIRTHDAY, PRINCE

THE TIMELINE

October 6, 1590: On the official 17th Birthday of the 3rd Earl of Southampton (the birthday of his official mother's "goodly boy"), Burghley informs him that he is a prince. He then exercises his guardian's right and proposes that the boy marry Elizabeth Vere, his granddaughter. Southampton says he needs time to think about it and Burghley grants him a year to make up his mind.

1590-1591: Oxford writes seventeen short poems to Southampton for his seventeenth birthday—all on the subject of Southampton having a son.

Southampton visits his friend the Earl of Rutland at Cambridge.

March to August 1591: He secretly travels to Dieppe, France, to confer with Lord Essex, who is busy fighting a war.

August 1591: The Queen is a guest of Southampton at his estate, Titchfield, for five days. During her visit LOVE'S LABOUR'S LOST is given its first performance by Oxford's Boys in a small park at Titchfield House.

THE STORY

When Henry Wriothesley, the 3rd Earl of Southampton, officially turns 17, his guardian, Lord Burghley, has big news for him. First: He is told that he is a royal prince, son of Elizabeth and Lord Oxford. Second: He is to marry Burghley's granddaughter, Elizabeth. It must be quite a surprise. He pleads for more time but Burghley is not accustomed to making accommodations. Southampton probably puts him over a barrel by pointing out that, since he has been using someone else's birthday all these years, he isn't actually seventeen yet. Burghley has no choice but to agree to the delay and hope that it won't spoil his master plan because, when Southampton marries his granddaughter and then becomes King, Burghley will become the Grandfather of a Queen. The Cecils will become royalty and their position will be secure.

Oxford and the Queen are behind the marriage plans along with Burghley. The boy is upset with his new-found parents because their plan involves letting the Cecils continue to be the power behind the throne and run England in the next reign, whereas Southampton and Essex have been plotting for years to take over the reins of government from the Cecils whom they believe are leading England into being a weak, second-rate country dependent on negotiation with Spain and France instead of a country strong in it's own right.

Elizabeth relies on a small clique of advisors, the most dominant of whom, Burghley and his son Robert Cecil, control the Privy Council and the Treasury, which gives them a very strong voice in her government.

The "out" party revolves around Essex and Southampton. Essex, as Elizabeth's favorite and protégé of her all-time favorite, Robert Dudley, thinks that, of course, she will take his advice. He believes that when Burghley finally dies, he (Essex), is the logical replacement to be Elizabeth's Principal Secretary. When spymaster Walsingham dies, both Cecil and Essex compete to provide the Foreign and domestic intelligence needed to keep England and Elizabeth safe. Essex sets out to prove the Queen is getting bad advice from the Cecils. To this end he hires the Bacon Brothers, Anthony and Francis, to advise him and spy for him. He also makes contact with King James of Scotland because it seems evident that Elizabeth could die at any moment, and there is no blood heir to the throne. Essex would like to be a power in whatever comes next.

After Southampton convinces Burghley to grant him a waiting period he immediately leaves to visit his friend the Earl of Rutland; probably in order to tell him what he has just discovered about himself. Then on to Dieppe in France to break the news to his close political friend, Essex, who is fighting a war there, and to discuss how this changes their future plans. If Southampton is a Tudor Prince then that changes everything. Now they won't have to play ball with the Cecils or James, whom they dislike and distrust.

Oxford, in order to argue his case with his son, who is mad at him for allowing the Cecils to call the shots, has to do it long distance, by messenger. Since the subject matter is a huge state secret and messengers can't be trusted, he puts his argument in the form of short poems or sonnets. He sends seventeen in all (it's Southampton's 17th birthday), each written in a cryptic language designed to be fully understandable only to those "in the know." Each is a variation on his basic message: "You are a Tudor prince. You owe it to your ancestors, your queen, your mother, your father, your people, and yourself to reproduce yourself—get married."

Sonnet 1:

From fairest creatures (Princes) *we desire increase,*
That thereby beauty's Rose (Elizabeth's Tudor Rose) *might*
    never die,
But as the riper should by time decease,
His tender heir might bear his memory:
But thou, contracted to thine own bright eyes,
Deed'st thy light's flame with self-substantial fuel,
Making a famine where abundance lies,
Thyself thy foe, to thy sweet (royal) *self too cruel.*
*Thou that art now the world's (*England's*) fresh ornament,*
And only herald to the gaudy spring,
Within thine own bud buriest thy content,
And, tender churl, mak'st waste in niggarding:
Pity the world, or else this glutton be,
To eat the world's due, by the grave and thee.

The pleading has no effect and Southampton gives
Burghley an answer of "no."

The Queen's visit to Tichfield, along with Burghley and
Oxford, is probably a personal effort on her part to use
whatever motherly charm she has to convince young
Southampton that, by herself, she's actually powerless to
make him a king. It can happen only with the help of her
Principal Secretary, Lord Burghley, who can vouch for the
secret marriage and the birth of the child and can grease the
wheels of Parliament to have him declared next in line.
And besides, Southampton surely will need the Cecil
expertise in order to run the government because no one
knows as much as the Cecils do about governing.
Burghley's price is a family alliance through his lovely
granddaughter, Elizabeth—a small price to pay and, of
course, using Robert Cecil as his Principal Secretary,

instead of the Earl of Essex. The Queen, now seriously old, feels she can't make it happen without Burghley.

During the queen's stay at Southampton's estate at Titchfield LOVE'S LABOURS LOST is given it's first performance by Oxford's Boys in a little park-like area outside the main house identical to the one in the play (the shrubbery is in all the right places, and Oxford obviously wrote it with that location in mind). The plot concerns a group of young men who, in their naïveté, believe they can get along without women. Then they meet the princess of France and her ladies and fall madly in love. The women don't trust their ardor and trick the men into revealing how shallow their love really is. Then the women pack up and leave with strict instructions to the men on how they must behave until they meet again in a year. Everything gets postponed. I believe Oxford may be suggesting that perhaps everyone should take a year off from any further talk of marriage—maybe attitudes will change. In any case, he must have thought the play carried an important message because it meant schlepping a whole company of boys, costumes, wigs and props 80 miles from London (a three day trip by carriage) for one performance. Southampton still doesn't budge, but maybe everyone takes the play's advice, because the year ahead brings no further attempts to change his mind.

CHAPTER 13

THE CREATION OF
THE PEN-NAME
"SHAKESPEARE"

THE TIMELINE

April 18, 1593: A long dramatic poem entitled VENUS AND ADONIS is registered and printed by Richard Field. Field is one of William Cecil's favorite printers and the manuscript has the approving stamp of the Archbishop himself. The name *"WILLIAM SHAKESPEARE" appears for the first time anywhere,* signing the dedication to the 3rd Earl of Southampton. VENUS AND ADONIS is based on Ovid's *Metamorphoses,* Book 10, well known to Oxford in the translation by Arthur Golding, his maternal uncle, who tutored him when he was a boy.

April 1593: There is a rumor going around that Southampton is going to be made a Knight of the Garter.

May 1593: George Peele writes THE HONOUR OF THE GARTER

May 1593: Essex campaigns hard to have Francis Bacon appointed Attorney General. Instead, Elizabeth appoints Burghley's choice, Sir Edward Coke.

July 1593: VENUS AND ADONIS is reprinted when the first edition of 1,250 copies sells out after only three months. (There were, at this time, only about 50,000 literate people in London out of a population of about 200,000.)

THE STORY

It is 1593 and ever since Southampton's 17th birthday two years ago, the Queen, Burghley and Oxford have been trying to get him to say "yes" to marrying Burghley's granddaughter. Oxford has written him 17 Sonnets that plead, beg and order him to reproduce. The Queen, with Oxford and Burghley, has visited him at Titchfield and tried to reason with him, mother to son, while Oxford's play LOVE'S LABOURS LOST, advises everyone to make no decision for a year. To top it off, Burghley has threatened him with a horrendous fine of £5,000 (Current value £1,181,000 / $1,725,440) if he won't marry her, but nothing seems to have any effect on the boy. However, the three of them have spent the last eighteen years of their lives on this Tudor Prince Project and they're not going to give up without one final effort.

They decide to try a new tack. If they can get Southampton to realize how much the people of England want and need a Tudor prince, who will guarantee a peaceful transition, maybe he will listen to the voice of the people, change his mind and marry Burghley's granddaughter. Oxford, as the propaganda expert, is drafted to write something special to tease the public into believing there might be a prince hiding away somewhere. He knows it must be something scandalous enough to get everyone's attention, mysterious enough to make them look beneath the surface for a hidden message and well written enough to impress readers with the knowledge of the writer. Burghley will arrange for the printing by one of his favorite printers, Richard Field, who can be trusted to be discreet about the provenance of the poem. The Archbishop himself will approve its publication, which will only heighten the intrigue. They prime the pump by floating rumors of Southampton being honored as a Knight of the Garter (in spite of his youth and lack of accomplishments). A poem, THE HONOR OF THE GARTER, is published celebrating Southampton by making a non-existent ancestor of his a founding member of the order. It's written by George Peele. (Which, I believe, is another pen-name of Oxford's).

The main effort is VENUS AND ADONIS (transparently, Elizabeth and Oxford) which tells, in sensuous detail, the story of the Goddess Venus who shamelessly seduces a handsome but young and naive Adonis, who only wants to be left alone to hunt wild boars (the boar being Oxford's family symbol). In the end, he is killed by a boar but from his blood on the ground is born a royal purple flower, and Venus speaks to it, *"Thou are next of blood and 'tis thy right."* It's an immaculate conception! Then she flies away in her chariot.

Up until now, Oxford has written practically everything anonymously. But such an explosive story about a royal prince can't come from an unknown author. It has to come from a person with a name. He can't use his own name because, after all, it's about him and the public mustn't know who is behind it. For such an important purpose he needs a name that sounds like it means something important. Anticipating Marshall McLuhan's advice to make the medium the message, he chooses "Shakespeare" probably for it's warrior-like connotation of shaking the spear of his pen for the great cause of putting his son, the 3rd Earl of Southampton, on the throne where he belongs because of his Tudor blood from Elizabeth. Possibly he chooses "William" because, ever since William the Conqueror, for whom his ancestors fought, the name William has meant "protector of the realm," and that's how he sees himself and his mission. Or maybe he chooses the name for other reasons entirely. It doesn't much matter because it works!

At least it works with the public. VENUS AND ADONIS hits the stands and the public eats it up. There's no question their curiosity is aroused. A Tudor Prince to succeed Elizabeth—really? The 1st edition quickly goes viral and, less than a year later, the first reprint is available.

It's a long erotic poem, very sensuous, with powerful political overtones: ten editions of 1250 copies each (the legal limit) by 1602. It arouses everyone's curiosity about Southampton and this writer Shakespeare, whoever he is. References to Queen Elizabeth are all over the poem and this guy Shakespeare seems to be saying that Southampton is her child and is therefore a Tudor prince. The dedication is to the 3rd Earl of Southampton and is as tantalizing as the poem:

> *"But if the first heire of my invention* (This poem written under my new pen-name) *prove deformed, I shall be sorie* (sorry) *it had so noble a god-father: and never after eare* (plow) *so barren a land, for fear it yield me still so bad a harvest. I leave it to your Honourable survey, and your Honour to your heart's content, which I wish may always*

answer your own wish, and the world's hopeful expectation.
Your Honors in all duty"— William Shakespeare.

The phrase, *"The world's hopeful expectation"* sounds like a euphemism for a prince. So does, *"Thou are next of blood and 'tis thy right."* The possibility of a Tudor prince of Elizabeth's blood is very exciting. Elizabeth is old and the English people are worried that, without a blood heir, it won't be a peaceful transition to the next reign—they fear civil war. James VI of Scotland is much gossiped about as a possible king, but many English dislike him, mostly because he's a Scot, and the English look down on the Scots. A Tudor prince would definitely avert a war. But who is this poet, William Shakespeare, who is saying that one exists? Can they believe him? No one seems to know, but book sales are going through the roof.

Whoever he is, his dedication seems to be saying that if this dramatic poem (written under the pen-name William Shakespeare) doesn't produce the desired result, he won't try again.

What result? Try to do what again? I believe it means that if this doesn't sway Southampton then Oxford promises to make no more attempts to convince him to take the crown on Burghley's terms.

CHAPTER 14

WILLIAM SHAGSPERE FROM STRATFORD JOINS THE STORY

THE TIMELINE

1551: John Shagspere (William's father, age 20) buys his early freedom from apprenticeship and sets up shop in Stratford as a glover. He is successful.

1557: John marries Mary Arden (19) , a young woman who has just inherited some property from her deceased father. He is immediately given the position of Official Ale Taster.

1558: Baby Joan is born but dies in infancy

1561: John is elected Chamberlain of the Borough of Stratford..

1562: Baby Margaret is born but dies 7 months later.

April 28, 1564: Baby *William Shagspere is christened* and John becomes an alderman of Stratford.

1569: He applies for a coat of arms to make him a gentleman, claiming his grandfather was a hero in the War of the Roses and was granted land by Henry VII in 1485. The Herald's Office turns him down.

1570: He becomes Chief Alderman (Mayor) of Stratford.

1570s: John Shagspere is prosecuted for illegal dealing in wool (brogging) and usury. He is accused of making loans worth £220 (2015 = £61,590) and charging 20 - 25% interest (Over 10% is considered usury and is illegal)

1576: Parliament forbids legal licensees (and broggers) from buying & selling wool for a period of eleven months. This is to keep English wool from being sold to Europe.

1579: John Shagspere, in financial difficulty, mortgages his wife's estate, Asbies, and takes in a paying tenant.

1580: John is fined £40 for missing a court date.

November 27,1582: William Shagspere gets engaged to Anne Whateley of Temple Grafton.

November 28,1582: William Shagspere (age 19) marries Ann Hathaway (age 26) of Shottery.

May 1583: Susanna Shagspere is christened

May 1583: John Shagspere's paying tenant takes him to court to get out of his lease. The tenant wins the case.

February 1585: The twins, Hamnet & Judith Shagspere are christened

1586: John Shagspere is removed from the Stratford Board of Aldermen.

1590: The Town of Stratford is in serious economic

distress. Bailiff William Parsons and the burgesses of Stratford petition Lord Burghley, in London, for relief.

1590: It is reported that John Shagspere's only possession is his house on Henley Street.

1592: John Shagspere is fined for not attending Church of England services (that makes him a "recusant" Catholic). He claims it is "for fear of process for debt," which is a typical plea from recusants.

August 1592: John Shagspere is hired to appraise the belongings of his old friend, Henry Field, recently deceased father of Richard Field, the London printer.

1593: A new law is passed: 'Recusant' Catholics are forbidden to travel more than five miles from their homes.

September 1594: Stratford is devastated by fire. Most of Henley Street is destroyed.

September 1595: Stratford is again devastated by fire. John Shagspere may have lost everything including the house on Henley St.

December 1595: Stratford again petitions the Crown for relief. One third of the population are paupers, there is a soaring death rate and vagrants are being denied entry to the town. Times are tough in Stratford.

THE STORY

Connecting these dots, It's not too hard to figure out that John Shagspere is a real go-getter. At age 20 he buys an early release from apprenticeship and sets up shop as a glover in Stratford. He does well, but you have to be a "head of household" to hold public office in Stratford. His fortuitous marriage to Mary Arden gives him property and greater stature in the town. Now he is a "head of household" and he is immediately made Official Ale Taster. His political career is off to a good start. After losing two girls in infancy he and Mary have their first male child, William, who survives. For thirteen years John thrives and rises in importance, finally becoming Chief Alderman (Mayor) of Stratford. Meanwhile, his business migrates from making gloves to brogging (illegal middleman selling wool wherever he can get the best price, including to Europe) and illegal lending of money. He buys two more houses on Henley Street. Broggers sell so much wool to Europe that textile makers all over England are starving for work. Parliament's solution is to forbid all wool sales by middlemen. They even collect a "hostage payment" in advance which will be forfeited in case of a violation. This essentially puts John out of business. His fortunes decline rapidly; in 1579 he has to mortgage his wife's property and take in a paying tenant in order to get by and also seems to be in some trouble with the court. He is also a Catholic and is missing compulsory attendance at Church of England services, thereby becoming a 'recusant'.

It's time for his son, William, now 19, to help the family out by following in his father's footsteps and marrying a woman of property. The bans are posted for him to marry a young woman from Temple Grafton named Anne Whateley, but before the ink is dry in the record book, he ditches his betrothed and marries Anne Hathaway of Shottery at a shotgun wedding. She is 26 and three months pregnant (which evidently trumps the posted banns in Temple Grafton). Expectant wife moves in with him and his parents on Henley street. After the birth, I suspect the house gets a little crowded and noisy because the tenant tries to break his lease. Shagspere takes him to court but loses the case, and the paying tenant moves out. This does not help the family finances very much.

The family's fortunes and stature continue to deteriorate and in 1586 John is removed from the Stratford Board of Aldermen. A new law restricting recusant Catholics to within five miles of their homes doesn't help matters because it restricts his economic activities to his home town, and Stratford is in dire straits due to the dying off of the yarn and clothing business. There is no work, and the Bailiff petitions Lord Burghley, in London, for relief: *"The said town is now fallen into much decay for want of such trade as heretofore they had by clothing and making yarn."*

John Shagspere gets a little temporary work appraising the property of his old friend, Henry Field, who has died. Henry's son, Richard, a successful London printer, probably visits Stratford at least once or twice while he settles his father's affairs and, of course, has dealings with John Shagspere who is functioning as appraiser. He probably also becomes reacquainted with William, who is only three years younger than he is and who seems to be having a hard time. Poor Will has three kids, little work, no money and still lives with his parents.

A few years later everything gets worse. In 1594 and 1595 Stratford is devastated by two enormous fires which burn out much of this Medieval, wooden town, including Henley Street and the streets nearby, not to mention that the years from 1594 to 1597 are famine years, and Stratford once again petitions the Crown for aid. The Shagsperes are having a hard time holding their heads above water and resort to hoarding grain illegally during the famine. Their only chance is for the boy, William, to go to London and look up his old friend, Richard Field, and see if he can help. After all, Richard is one of London's most respected printers, he must have some useful connections and Stratford, at the moment, is a dead end.

CHAPTER 15

"SHAKESPEARE" DECLARES WAR ON THE CECILS

THE TIMELINE

November 1590: Elizabeth's Accession Day celebrations saw the idea of the 'Virgin Queen', first put forth in 1578 in an entertainment designed by the poet Thomas Churchyard, move towards a fully fledged 'cult' of *Gloriana*. It was a magnificent ceremony that sought to deify the post-menopausal queen both as a 'Vestal Virgin' and as a goddess incarnate. As a vestal maiden she could be both pure and sexually alluring, but as a goddess she was a 'Virgin Mother,' a second Madonna, "whom neither time nor age can wither" (see *Elizabeth* (2016) by John Guy, pg. 145).

May 1594: THE RAPE OF LUCRECE, another long dramatic poem by William Shakespeare and also dedicated to the 3rd Earl of Southampton is printed by Richard Field and published by John Harrison.

November 1594: Southampton pays £5,000 (current value £1,181,000 / $1,725,440) to Burghley as a penalty for <u>not</u> marrying his granddaughter.

January 1595: The 3rd edition of VENUS AND ADONIS is published.

January 1595: RICHARD II (anonymous) is performed for the first time by The Chamberlain's Men. It's about Richard II handing over his crown to Bolingbroke.

1595: "The year saw the handsome young Earl of Southampton (21) emerging at the Court of QE as a budding favorite who might well replace Essex."— Akrigg.

THE STORY

Southampton ignores the public fuss caused by VENUS AND ADONIS and continues to say, "No" to marrying Cecil's granddaughter. The public has been aroused for nothing.

Oxford, true to his promise to *"never again eare so barren a land,"* writes THE RAPE OF LUCRECE, a story easily deciphered as an attack on the Cecils by "Shakespeare" with an even more tantalizing dedication to Southampton:

> *"The Love I dedicate to your Lordship is without end: whereof this Pamphlet without beginning is but a superfluous Moiety* (part). *...What I have done is yours, what I have to do is yours, being part in all I have, devoted yours. Were my worth greater, my duty would show greater; meantime, as it is, it is bound to your Lordship, to whom I wish long life, still lengthened with all happinesse."-William Shakespeare*

It sounds even more like Shakespeare is addressing Southampton as his king, this time promising to support him in all his endeavors. But why is he telling this particular story?

THE RAPE OF LUCRECE is a retelling of the tragedy of Lucrece made famous by Livy and Ovid wherein a young Roman officer named Collatine has bragged so much about the virtue of his wife, Lucrece, that the evil, morally weak, Sextus Tarquinius, son of Emperor Lucius

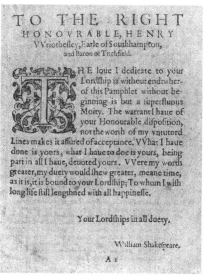

Fig. 6 - The Dedication to Southampton in the 1594 edition of Lucrece.

Tarquinius, is tempted to "have his way" with her. By force, if necessary. He tricks his way into her bedroom and forces her into a compromising position. She's faced with a hard choice: He tells her that if she resists the rape both she and a servant will die and the servant will be blamed. If she doesn't resist, Tarquin promises he will be her "secret friend." That would save her own life and that of the servant but risks bearing Tarquin's child and bringing eternal shame on her family. She chooses a third way: She doesn't resist, but next day summons her husband, her father and the whole army to hear her charges against

Sextus Tarquinius and swear them to avenge her honor. Whereupon, she commits suicide.

At the end, Brutus who, up till now, has been regarded as a fool, takes charge and declares that Lucrece was wrong. She should have fought for her virtue. Then he reprimands Collatine and his father-in-law for wasting their energy feeling sorry for themselves instead of taking action and going to the people to show them the extent of the crime and drive the Tarquins out. They take his advice and, as a result, the Tarquins are exiled and the Roman government is overthrown and changed from kings to consuls.

The "in" crowd would recognize Elizabeth as Lucrece, not to mention Burghley and his son Robert Cecil, as the Tarquins, pere and fils. The poem refers several times to Lucrece in terms of red and white images familiar to everyone as the colors of the Tudor Dynasty. Her life and her dynasty are tied up together, and it can be seen that Oxford, like Collatine, is regretting his part in glorifying Queen Elizabeth as England's "Virgin Queen," competing with the Catholic Virgin Mary and helping to create the whole cult of "Gloriana," which everyone, especially Elizabeth herself, buys into. This romantic fantasy is proving to be yet another obstacle to proclaiming a Tudor prince.

Once Southampton pays Burghley the £5,000 penalty the marriage question and the Tudor Prince problem is over as far as the Cecils are concerned. But that leaves the question of who will actually succeed to the throne. Recently, Elizabeth has been treating Southampton with special favor. What if she tries to put her son on the throne without the Cecils? To counter this possibility, they must persuade her that it would be better without Southampton. Their argument is that if she admits publicly she has a son, she may save the Tudor dynasty, but she will have to give up the title of "Virgin Queen" and the whole "Gloriana" fairytale to which she has become quite firmly attached. Her conflict is between her duty to her Tudor Dynasty and her vanity. Vanity wins. The Cecils convince her that her legacy will be even greater as "Virgin Queen Elizabeth, the last of the Tudors." They'll make sure of it. After she dies, Robert Cecil will engineer a smooth transfer of power to James, and he will make sure Elizabeth will be revered forever as "England's Virgin Queen." Which is exactly what happens. Even today, most people think of her as The Virgin Queen and can become quite upset at any suggestion that it might not be literally true.

Oxford, like Brutus, believes she should not give in to the Cecils but fight to save the Tudor dynasty. His entire adult life has been spent preparing for his son to take his place on the throne of England and carry on the dynastic name of Tudor. At the end of Lucrece, he is telling Southampton that it's up to the two of them to save the Dynasty by exposing the Cecils as traitors to the Tudor Throne and driving them from government. Essentially, he is declaring war on the Cecils. Which means that, between the writing of "VENUS AND ADONIS" and "THE RAPE OF LUCRECE," Oxford has changed political sides. As he says in the dedication,

"What I have done is yours, what I have to do is yours, being part in all I have, devoted yours"

This tells the public that "William Shakespeare" (whoever he is) thinks Southampton is a Tudor prince who should be king and that he (Shakespeare) will support him in whatever course he takes and, by extension, so should everyone else. It lets Southampton know that his father has stopped trying to get him to play ball with the Cecils and will now be an active supporter of the opposition party led by himself and the Earl of Essex. It also lets the public know that they should follow Southampton and Essex. The enemy is the Cecils. But they still want to know who is this man Shakespeare—can we believe him?

CHAPTER 16

ROBERT CECIL FIGHTS BACK

THE TIMELINE

March 1595: "Shakespeare" (authorial spelling) is listed, along with William Kempe and Richard Burbage, as one of the 3 payees of the newly formed Chamberlains Men for performances at Court the previous December. *This is the first historical mention of the name "Shakespeare" in connection with anything theatrical.*

July 1596: Robert Cecil becomes Principal Secretary, thereby cutting off Essex. Now he is officially running the Secret Service. There has been and continues to be a battle between Cecil & Essex for the Queen's ear.

October 1596: Francis Bacon warns Essex that Robert Cecil is plotting his downfall.

October 1596: William Shagspere of Stratford applies to the Herald's office to grant his father the coat of arms they refused to give him 28 years ago. They grant the request on payment of £30 (Current value: £5,274/$7,705). Who paid that? The motto on the shield says, "Not Without Right."

January 1597: RICHARD II (anonymous) is published.

May 1597: Shagspere buys New Place, the second largest house in Stratford from a William Underhill for £60. (Where did he get the money?)

July 1597: A play, THE ISLE OF DOGS by Ben Jonson and Thomas Nashe (another pen-name of Oxford's?), is performed at the Swan and suppressed after causing great offence to the government. (**"contanynge very seditious & sclandrous matter"**). The script is totally lost to history, but there was a real island in the Thames where the Queen kenneled her dogs and it was also where the Privy Council met. (The comedic possibilities are obvious.) It must have really hit a political nerve because arrest warrants are issued for three of the players (**Gabriel Spenser, Robert Shaw, and Ben Jonson**), and Cecil closes every theatre in London. Jonson and Spenser are jailed in Marshalsea Prison for a couple of months, but history tells us that Thomas Nashe escapes to Great Yarmouth and is never punished.

1598: Ben Jonson is back in prison for killing his fellow actor Gabriel Spenser (did he blame Spenser for his imprisonment?). He escapes execution for murder by pleading "benefit of Clergy" (proves he can read Latin). He converts to Catholicism, a convict's brand is burned on his thumb and he is released.

December 1598: THE THEATRE is torn down and the wood is used to build THE GLOBE

February 1598: William Shagspere is cited for hoarding grain in a famine year. He is listed in official records as a resident of New Place, in Stratford.

February 1598: Southampton and Robert Cecil make an official visit to France. Southampton is "presented" to the French King.

August 1598: Burghley dies at 77. His son, Robert Cecil, takes over as advisor to the Queen, cutting out Essex.

September 1598: PALLADIS TAMIA is published by Francis Meres. It's a sort of catalogue of contemporary writing and art, and it connects the name "Shakespeare" as author to 12 plays beloved by audiences and previously published with no name on the title page.

October 1598: RICHARD II & RICHARD III are republished with "Shakespeare" named as author.

January 1599: EVERY MAN OUT OF HIS HUMOUR by Ben Jonson containing the character of Sogliardo is acted by The Chamberlains men at the CURTAIN Theatre (a temporary home while the GLOBE is being built).

April 1599: Oxford writes a speech praising Essex which is inserted into HENRY V, by Shakespeare, currently performing at THE CURTAIN.

May 1599: THE GLOBE Theater is finished. "Shakespeare" (authorial spelling) owns a 1/10 interest in it.

THE STORY

The publishing of RAPE OF LUCRECE must have caught Robert Cecil off guard, but I'm sure he lost no time in having a talk with Richard Field about not printing anything else written by William Shakespeare. Maybe I'm abusing my artistic license, but I can easily imagine that Richard, hoping to lighten things up, comments on the amusing similarity in name between the author of the two long poems he has printed and an illiterate young man from his hometown of Stratford who, by the way, happens to be in London.

This is the break Robert Cecil has been waiting for. This is no laughing matter. He has just struck gold! If he can get the public to believe that the spokesman in opposition to Cecil is actually a nobody who just blew in from Stratford he will have solved a major problem, perhaps even prevented a civil war. No matter that the man's documented name is Shaxsper or Shagspere or sometimes Shaksper—it's close enough for government work. The fact that the man is illiterate may actually be an advantage because it means he won't leave a paper trail of his own. If possible, Cecil will keep Shagspere, himself, in the dark. It should be easy to convince him that the Queen can use his services as her eyes and ears in Stratford. Essentially, Cecil will pretend to hire him as a spy. Shagspere's only real job is to stay alive and available while Cecil figures out exactly how to use him. The first thing Cecil does is to establish a phony ID. He creates a phony receipt to William Kempe, Richard Burbage and "Shakespeare" (authorial spelling) as payees of the newly formed Chamberlain's Men for performances at Court the previous December. The first two are well known members of that company of actors, but there is no evidence that there ever was a real actor named William Shakespeare attached to the Chamberlain's Men and certainly not important enough to be the receiver of company payroll; however, Shagspere now has his first theatrical credit.

What's in it for Shagspere? Quite a bit. I don't believe that, at first, he knew the real reason for the government's sudden interest in him but, being good at bargaining, he makes a pretty good one with Cecil. The first thing he gets—a coat of arms for his father—costs Cecil the filing fee (or bribe?) of £30 (current value $7,705) to the office of the Herald. (*In 1602 a complaint is filed against the Herald for mis-approving 23 coats of arms, including John Shagspere's*). Shagspere's father becomes the gentleman he always wanted to be and eventually is put back on the Stratford town council. Only seven months later William has enough money to buy New Place in Stratford, from the well-connected William Underhill for £60 (over $15,000 current value). Underhill is the son of Sir William Hatton, first husband of Elizabeth Hatton, wife of Edward Coke, appointed Attorney General of England only four years ago and Cecil's man. Maybe this connection to Cecil is coincidental, but I don't believe it. Built of brick since the great fires two years ago, New Place is the second biggest house in town containing 20 rooms and 10 fireplaces. (Was it used as an Inn? It certainly would have needed a staff.) William and his father move in. The Shagsperes' fortunes have definitely taken a turn for the better.

In spite of their recent good fortune, his past catches up to him and, in 1598, William is cited for "hoarding grain in a famine."

In 1598 William Cecil, Lord Burghley, father-in-law to Oxford, dies of old age. Almost immediately, Francis Meres publishes his compendium of philosophy, music, painting and literature named PALLADIS TAMIA (Wits Treasury) which informs the reading public that "Shakespeare" is the man who wrote a dozen of their favorite plays which they have found so inspirational and he lists them. It compares him to Ovid and links him as a comic writer to: *Comedy of Errors*; *Two Gentlemen of Verona*; *Love Labours Lost*; *Love Labours Won*; *Midsummers Nights Dream* and *The Merchant of Venice*. And for tragedy to: *Richard II*; *Richard III*; *Henry the IV*; *King John*; *Titus Andronicus* and *Romeo & Juliet*.

Frances Meres just happens to be the brother-in-law of John Florio, who is the famous Italian translator who has worked with Oxford and has lived with and taught Oxford's princely son, the 3rd Earl of Southampton. It appears that now that his father-in-law is dead, Oxford is bringing the battle over the name out in the open and Frances Meres helps him (wittingly or not) in his effort to connect his famous works with his now-famous pen-name in the public mind. The war to control the name "Shakespeare" is declared!

PALLADIS TAMIA is immediately followed by the republishing of RICHARD II & RICHARD III, now credited to "Shakespeare." It's an indication of how incendiary things are becoming. The first play obviously refers to Elizabeth handing over her crown and the second slanders Robert Cecil by satirizing his deformity and turning him into hunch-backed Richard III, the man from whom the Tudors took the crown, painting him as a monster. Oxford wants the public to know whose side "Shakespeare" is on.

This is followed by a speech which Oxford writes and inserts in HENRY V, now in performance at the Curtain Theatre, rousing the audience to support Essex as he leaves for Ireland with Southampton at the head of 15,000 men to pacify Ireland once and for all.

Were now the general of our gracious empress
(As in good time he may) from Ireland coming,
Bringing rebellion broached on his sword,

How many would the peaceful city quit to welcome him!

There's no question—"Shakespeare" is rooting for Essex and a battle is on between Oxford and Robert Cecil over who will control the name, "Shakespeare." Oxford will try and convince the public that "Shakespeare" is an important political figure who knows a lot about Court politics and that's why he's saying all those terrible things about the Cecils. Cecil will try and pin the name on a real, but illiterate, pretend actor in the Chamberlain's Men (Oxford's company) who has no political knowledge or importance.

MEANWHILE:

In May 1599 THE GLOBE Theater is finished. The Burbage brothers, Richard and Cuthbert, own half of the lease. The other half is split 5 ways between Heminge, Phillips, Pope, Kempe and "Shakespeare." I suspect that this is Cecil, busy establishing an identity and a salary for Shagspere that won't have to be paid by the crown. However, when Shagspere dies in 1616 there is no mention of Globe shares in his will, so perhaps Cecil actually owned them. In any case, by 1599 Shagspere had figured out the truth about his employment and was taking every advantage he could, including peddling scurrilous versions of Shakespeare's plays to fly-by-night printers. I can easily imagine Oxford suggesting to Ben Jonson, an unemployed writer, that he might write a comedy about the situation. He (Oxford) would make sure it got produced. No writer could resist that offer and EVERY MAN OUT OF HIS HUMOUR is the result, which was performed at the CURTAIN (before THE GLOBE was finished).

The play contains the character of Sogliardo, who is ridiculed for having gotten a coat of arms showing a boar without a head.

> SOGLIARDO: . . . .*how like you the crest, sir?*
> PUNTARVOLO: *I understand it not well, what is't?*
> SOGLIARDO: *Marry, sir, it is your boar without a head, rampant* (standing on its hind legs with it's forefeet in the air). *A boar without a head, that's very rare!*
> CARLO BUFFONE: *Ay, and rampant too! Troth, I commend the herald's wit, he has deciphered him well: a swine without a head, without brain, wit, anything indeed, ramping to gentility.*

Many Oxfordians, myself included, believe that Jonson's character, Sogliardo, is a satire on the Stratford man (Shagspere) passing himself off as Shakespeare (Oxford), the writer, because the 17th Earl of Oxford's crest is a boar. In other words, Sogliardo's crest is Oxford without his head (the creative part). This leads me to believe that, by this time, Shagspere had figured out the scheme and his place in it and was exploiting it. Oxford and Jonson are trying to subversively expose what is going on. The battle for the name isn't over yet.

CHAPTER 17

THE ESSEX REBELLION

THE TIMELINE

May 1599: Essex has been sent to Ireland with 15,000 men to defeat Tyrone and finally bring an end to the endless Irish rebellion. He appoints Southampton Master of the Horse against the Queen's stated wishes.

August 1599: Amid fears of another Spanish invasion and rumors that King James VI of Scotland is ready to support a Catholic uprising, chains are drawn across London streets, and it is reported that the Queen is dangerously ill.

September 1599: Alone, in the middle of a river in Ireland, Essex makes a truce with Tyrone. The Queen orders him to revoke it and fight to the death.

September 1599: Essex, Southampton & Danvers ride three days and nights to see the Queen personally at Nonesuch Palace. Essex is placed under house arrest.

September 21, 1599: First performance of JULIUS CAESAR at The GLOBE by Chamberlain's Men (Rowse) (A play about conspiracy and civil war).

November 1599: The Privy Council proclaims an official denunciation of Essex at Nonesuch Palace—but still no trial or sentence.

December 1599: Essex, ever the "bad-boy" but still the "favorite," becomes so sick Elizabeth sends six of her own physicians. There are rumors of his death and funeral bells ring throughout London.

March 1600: Essex womenfolk are ordered out of Essex house, and the Earl is moved back in under the supervision of Robert Berkeley. Lady Essex is allowed to visit occasionally.

August 1600: Essex is finally set free but with severe restrictions—he must never come to Court.

December 1600: Essex & Southampton send a secret letter to King James VI of Scotland detailing wrongs done to them by Cecil and saying that they are going to try to wrest control from him.

February 7, 1601: three of Essex's supporters pay The Chamberlain's Men for a special performance of RICHARD II to be performed at the GLOBE with a new deposition scene showing the actual passing of the crown.

February 8, 1601: Essex Rebellion: It's a disaster and Southampton & Essex are sent to the Tower.

THE STORY

In Ireland, Essex appoints Southampton Master of the Horse in spite of Elizabeth's express wish that he not have any position at all. (Since the Prince won't play ball with the Queen, she won't play with him either—she's angry.)

The fighting doesn't go well, and Essex sees no way out except to make a truce with Tyrone. Elizabeth is furious and commands him to break the truce and fight to the death. Convinced that she is captive to bad advice from Cecil and other enemies far from the battlefield but close to the throne, he and Southampton cross back from Ireland to England and ride three days and nights to reach Nonesuch Palace and speak personally to the Queen. They succeed in frightening her half to death and driving her closer to Robert Cecil. On his advice, she bans them from her presence (they never see her again), puts Essex under arrest in York House and sets a court of inquiry to investigate him for treason. He becomes very ill and, amid rumors that he is dead, church bells ring out all over London and crowds gather. Spenser had called him "Great England's glory and the world's wide wonder" (in his poem "Prothalamion," line 146). His popularity could be dangerous! The power struggle is coming to a head.

Essex is finally freed and returns to Essex House. It becomes like a shadow court with Essex, Southampton and their followers meeting regularly to try to plan how to stage what might be called "an aristocratic intervention at court" The plan is to lead a large delegation of lords into the queen's presence and "humbly" petition her for the arrest of Robert Cecil, Lord Cobham and Sir Walter Raleigh, the earl's enemies, on charges of treason and corruption. (see "Shakespeare's *Richard II* and the Essex Rising" (2008) by Paul Hammer). Also, they want her to publically designate her heir and rid England of the fear of Civil War which is taking hold.

They decide to stage their "intervention" on February 14. They pay for a performance of an old play, RICHARD II, now widely known to be by Cecil's enemy, "Shakespeare," to be given a week before that, on February

7, because it demonstrates just such a peaceful handing over of power as well an object lesson in what can go wrong.

The play is about a ruler handing over his crown, which is what they want Elizabeth to do. Oxford has written a

Fig. 7 - Earl of Southampton in the Tower, circa 1601-1603.

scene never before performed, wherein Richard physically hands over his crown to Bolingbroke—the Deposition Scene. In the pre-rebellion version of this play the actual handing over of the crown is done off-stage. As every theatre person knows, one action is worth a thousand words, so I believe that, in order to focus on the peaceful and co-operative aspect of the desired transfer of power, "Shakespeare" (Oxford), re-writes the scene to bring the actual handing over of the crown right onstage where it will make a greater impression on the men who will be doing the same thing in just a week's time and possibly influence how the rest of the audience will view their actions.

The plan is to have a great lunch, see the play and spend the week making final preparations. In the event, they have the meal and attend the play, but when they return to Essex House, a messenger arrives with a request for Essex to come to the Privy Council and discuss new intelligence re: a new Spanish Armada. Suspecting a Cecil trap (correctly), Essex says, "No." The messenger leaves and, early the next day, an official delegation commands Essex's attendance. He totally panics, resulting in chaos and ignominious defeat. Southampton and Essex are imprisoned in the Tower of London. The famous Essex Rebellion (which was never supposed to be a rebellion) is over before it can begin. (see Hammer)

Oxford, involved, but not charged, is devastated. I'm sure he pulls every string he can but the first night his son spends in the Tower he writes: (see Whittemore)

Sonnet 27:

Weary with toil I haste me to my bed
The dear repose for limbs with travail tired,
But then begins a journey in my head,
To work my mind when body's work's expired.

For then my thoughts (from far where I abide)
Intend a zealous pilgrimage to thee,
And keep my drooping eye-lids open wide,
Looking on darkness, which the blind do see.

Save that my soul's imaginary sight
Presents thy shadow to my sightless view,
Which like a jewel (hung in ghastly night)
Makes black night beauteous, and her old face new.

CHAPTER 18

THE BARGAIN

THE TIMELINE

February 19,1601: A jury of peers is convened with Oxford (of all people) sitting at the head as befits his position as Lord Great Chamberlain. The conviction of Essex and Southampton is pre-ordained, and they are both sentenced to be gruesomely hanged, drawn and quartered.

February 25, 1601: Essex is executed.

March 19, 1601: Southampton's life is spared but he remains in the Tower. History has recorded no explanation.

THE STORY

Southampton and Essex are considered the ring-leaders and are convicted of treason. They are sentenced to be hanged, drawn and quartered. As a courtesy to his nobility, Essex has his head chopped off instead.

Oxford has a hereditary obligation to head up the jury and rule against his son, but now he tells the boy how he's going to help him by bargaining with his brother-in-law Robert Cecil.

Sonnet 35:

For to thy sensual fault I bring in sense –
Thy adverse party is thy advocate –
And 'gainst myself a lawful plea commence.

He continues writing sonnets as a way of communicating with his son in the Tower without the guards catching on. They are thoughtful, informative and poetic, with references to Southampton's royal status scattered throughout, made to look like a collection of brief love poems to nameless people. In the 1609 published version they are numbered, which means it must be important to Oxford that they are to be read in a particular order. This order turns out to be calendar order, as Hank Whittemore has discovered, which makes it a sort of secret diary of his son's stay in the Tower of London. We know this diary by its usual name of SHAKE-SPEARES SONNETS. [Whittemore's *The Monument* (2005) does a brilliant job of analyzing exactly how this was accomplished. I encourage you to read it. Once you can hear the messages buried in these "little songs" the rest of the pieces fall into place.]

March 19, 1601 Southampton's life is spared, although he remains in the Tower. No official explanation is given. However, according to the Sonnets, a bargain has been struck among Oxford, his brother-in-law Robert Cecil, King James VI of Scotland and Southampton. In return for Southampton's life, Oxford and his son promise to co-operate with Cecil's efforts to put James VI on the throne of England, stop the battle over the name "Shakespeare" and sever forever the connections between "Shakespeare," Oxford, the Queen and Southampton. He tells his son the terms of his bargain with Cecil:

Sonnet 36:

Let me confess that we two must be twain,
Although our un-divided loves are one—
So shall those blots that do with me remain
Without thy help be borne by me alone...

I may not ever-more acknowledge thee,
Lest my bewailed guilt should do thee shame,
Nor thou with public kindness honor me,
Unless thou take that honor from thy name!

Oxford's sonnet diary tells us what History has left out. In return for severing their connection, Southampton's life is spared by downgrading the charge from "Treason" to "Misprision of Treason" (i.e., he knew about it but didn't participate). In addition, upon Elizabeth's death, Southampton will be freed and made whole again, but the dream of him becoming king is over.

Sonnet 87:

*So thy great gift, upon **misprision** growing*
Comes home again, on better judgment making.
Thus have I had thee as a dream doth flatter:
In sleep a King, but waking no such matter.

CHAPTER 19

SOUTHAMPTON REGAINS HIS FREEDOM

THE TIMELINE

March 24, 1603: QUEEN ELIZABETH dies and Robert Cecil announces that James VI of Scotland will succeed her.

April 5, 1603: Only twelve days after Elizabeth's death, King James, still in Scotland, and *as his first official act*, sends an order freeing Southampton.

April 28, 1603: Queen Elizabeth's funeral (the Tudors are now officially finished).

May 16, 1603: Southampton receives a royal pardon from King James.

July 7, 1603: Southampton is appointed Captain of the Isle of Wight.

July 9, 1603: Southampton is made a Knight of the Garter.

July 21, 1603: Southampton is made an Earl again and his estate is returned to him.

1604: Expanded "true and perfect" version of HAMLET (too long to perform and believed by many to be practically Oxford's autobiography) is published.

March 15, 1604: King James stages a state procession through London. Southampton and his official mother are prominently displayed together.

May 17, 1604: The Chamberlain's Men become The King's Men.

June 24, 1604: Oxford dies in Hackney and Southampton is immediately thrown into the Tower of London overnight while his papers are searched.

THE STORY

Everyone sticks to the bargain. When Elizabeth dies, Southampton is immediately freed and soon his title and estate are returned to him by King James. In addition he is made a Knight of the Garter and given the small Isle of Wight to rule over. This is recorded in SHAKE-SPEARES SONNETS by Edward de Vere, 17th Earl of Oxford.

Sonnet 106:

When in the chronicle of wasted time,
*I see descriptions of the fairest **wights**,*
And beauty making beautiful old rhyme,
*In praise of ladies dead and lovely **knights**!*
………
For we which now behold these present days,
Have eyes to wonder, but lack tongues to praise!

113

All of this is strong evidence that both Southampton and Oxford were much more important people than history has recorded. Oxford's sonnet diary spells it out.

Sonnet 107:

The mortal moon hath her eclipse endur'd, (Elizabeth is dead)
And the sad augurs mock their own presage, (the nay-sayers were wrong)
Incertainties (James) *now crown themselves assur'd,*
And peace proclaims olives of endless age. (Civil war is averted)
Now with the drops of this most balmy time
My love (my son) *looks fresh, and Death to me subscribes,* (I've beaten the Grim Reaper)
Since spite of him I'll live in this poor rhyme,
While he insults o'er dull and speechless tribes; (I'll live in this poetry while he lectures the dead)
And thou (Southampton) *in this* (this diary) *shalt find thy monument,*
When tyrants' crests and tombs of brass are spent.

King James makes a great show of solidarity and gratitude by rewarding Southampton and making a fuss over Shakespeare's plays, continuing to pay Oxford's £1,000 annuity and giving him his much-claimed Forest of Waltham. In the royal parade, I don't think it's an accident that Southampton and his official mother are featured together. It's just Cecil making sure that everyone identifies her, not Queen Elizabeth, as his mother. The Chamberlain's Men, now on the royal payroll as The Kings Men, are also in the procession as a show of gratitude to Oxford. Also it shows that Oxford, knowing his end is near, is taking care of his actors and wrapping up the loose ends of his life.

In June of 1604 Oxford dies, whereupon Southampton is held overnight in The Tower while his papers are examined by the authorities. (We know this only from the reports of foreign diplomats—official English history doesn't mention it.) James must have worried that, without the father, would the son keep the bargain? True to Shakespeare's predictions regarding his own death, no one knows where Oxford's remains are placed. He simply vanishes.

Cecil has managed to neutralize the name "Shakespeare" and has thereby scotched the rumors that Shakespeare is someone important who knows that Southampton is the son of Queen Elizabeth. He has finally won the battle for the name. Or has he? It appears that Oxford has an ace up his sleeve. Before he dies he manages to smuggle his complete treasonous sonnet diary to Southampton. The bargain with Cecil was to permanently sever *all* connections (they were forbidden to even speak to each other). In Sonnet 74 Oxford tells his son that he is leaving the sonnets with him so he will be reminded of his royal roots.

Sonnet 74:

My life hath in this line some interest,
Which for memorial still with thee shall stay
When thou reviewest this, thou dost review
The very part was consecrate to thee:

The worth of that, is that which it contains,
And that is this, and this with thee remains.

In Sonnet 122 he tells him that he doesn't need the original (the only) copy since it is etched in his memory.

Sonnet 122:

Thy gift, thy tables, are within my brain
Full character'd with lasting memory,
Which shall above that idle rank remain
Beyond all date, even to eternity;
Or at the least, so long as brain and heart
Have faculty by nature to subsist.
Till each to raz'd oblivion yield his part
Of thee, thy record never can be miss'd.
That poor retention could not so much hold,
Nor need I tallies thy dear love to score;
Therefore to give them from me was I bold,
To trust those tables that receive thee more:
To keep an adjunct to remember thee
Were to import forgetfulness in me.

CHAPTER 20

SHAKE-SPEARES SONNETS & THE FIRST FOLIO

THE TIMELINE

1603: With James as King and Oxford dead, the Court's taste in entertainment changes and Ben Jonson jumps on the bandwagon writing the newest, popular art form: masques, for James's court. These are not plays but themed spectacles containing drama, music, dance and spectacular sets that "do things" performed by noble/royal amateurs. He writes about two dozen masques for James' court which gets him the artistic and financial recognition he couldn't get from Elizabeth's court.

1605: Ben writes MASQUE OF BLACKNESS with Susan Vere (Oxford's youngest daughter) performing in it. During that same period Susan marries Philip Herbert, Earl of Montgomery, Knight of the Garter and Gentleman of the King's Privy Chamber.

1605: The Gunpowder Plot to overthrow James and put his nine-year old daughter, Elizabeth, on the throne in his place is foiled by Cecil, evidently with help from Jonson.

July 1605: Shagspere buys interest-paying investments in Stratford for £440 (Present value: £87,630 / $127,953).

1607: Between 1604 & 1610 a parliamentary group led by the Earl of Southampton defeats the king's plans for Union with Scotland.

1608: Robert Cecil becomes Lord Treasurer, taking over the finances of England.

1609: VENUS & ADONIS is in its 5th edition; RAPE OF LUCRECE is in its 4th edition.

1609: SHAKE-SPEARE'S SONNETS is published.

1610: Ben Jonson becomes a Protestant again.

1612: Robert Cecil dies. Ben Jonson's opinion is, "He never cared for any man longer nor (than) he could make use of him."

1612: Popular Prince Henry dies leaving not-so-popular Prince Charles next in line.

1614: Jonson writes a Masque, THE GOLDEN AGE RESTORED (Elizabeth's reign was known as "The Golden Age"), starring the King's homosexual favorite, Lord Buckingham.

1615-1616: Jonson's own 1st Folio, THE WORKS OF BENJAMIN JONSON, is published, meticulously overseen by Ben himself.

1616: Jonson receives a pension of £66/yr (present value £11,240/$16,412) and becomes the first Poet Laureate. He stops writing plays.

1616: William Shagspere from Stratford dies. No one notices or says anything about him being a writer.

1617: The Venetian Ambassador reports home that King James doesn't trust Southampton.

1619: King James grants Southampton £1,200/yr in lieu of land.

1620: King James takes away income from sweet wines from Southampton.

1621: Southampton and Henry Vere (Oxford's son by his second wife, Elizabeth Trentham) are imprisoned for plotting with Edward Sandys in the House of Commons.

1623: Likelihood of a peaceful succession is in doubt.

1623: THE FIRST FOLIO is published.

THE STORY

It appears that, in order to get out of jail, Ben Jonson becomes an informant for Cecil. He "converts" to Catholicism and is released with a branded thumb. This will give him "authenticity" and make it easier for him to infiltrate the Catholic underground. Anti-James feelings are rising and subversion is everywhere. The Gunpowder Plot (to make James' nine year old daughter, Elizabeth, queen) fails and Jonson appears to have acted as a spy for Cecil. He is present at a supper party attended by one of the Gunpowder Plot conspirators and, after the plot's discovery, he volunteers what he knows of the affair to the investigator, Robert Cecil, and the Privy Council. He is not jailed.

As a member of the House of Lords, Southampton is politically active, working against King James and succeeding in killing the King's plan to join England and Scotland together. In secret, he manages to get SHAKE-SPEARES SONNETS published in hopes of influencing the next succession by letting the world know that James has usurped the throne from a Prince of Tudor blood. Shakespeare's two long dramatic poems, VENUS & ADONIS and RAPE OF LUCRECE are enjoying continuing popularity, as are the plays, so it's logical to expect that publishing SHAKE-SPEARES SONNETS will make a big noise and shake the foundations of James's government. Instead, there is a big silence. A huge non-event! It just vanishes without a trace! *It's hard to believe, but there is not one authentic contemporary record of anyone ever having bought, read or even heard of this dangerous book of sonnets. It's astonishing!* It appears that, once again, Cecil knows everything that's going on and confiscates all 1250 printed copies (maximum printing run) before they can be sold and has them destroyed. (400 years later we have found only 13 copies he missed, and they look like they've never been read but stashed away somewhere.)

Cecil realizes that, even though he has succeeded in preventing the sonnets and their "Southampton-is-a-Tudor-Prince" message from being read, it's obvious that, in spite of Oxford being dead, the name "Shakespeare" is still dangerous and capable of doing serious political damage to the royal interests. He has to find a way to permanently separate "Shakespeare" from Oxford and Southampton.

He makes Ben Jonson (Oxford's friend) a tempting offer he can't refuse: Jonson will be the editor of a huge folio edition of Shakespeare's Collected Plays—only the plays. The poems, VENUS & ADONIS and RAPE OF LUCRECE, with their dedications to Southampton, **will not be included**. The plays will be printed "as written" but the outer "packaging" will make it look like that guy Shagspere, the man from Stratford, wrote the plays. In exchange, the Crown will pay to publish the giant folio of Jonson's THE WORKS OF BENJAMIN JONSON, a unique and expensive project he's been dreaming about for years.

Cecil's death in 1612 interrupts things and someone new must be found to take charge. Jonson's connection with Buckingham and Elizabeth Vere is the perfect conduit to the two brothers, Philip and William Herbert, two important men in James' government who have a strong interest in a peaceful succession for Prince Charles. A deal is made, and Jonson immediately sets about bringing out his own **complete** WORKS just about the same time that Shagspere of Stratford dies in 1616. It is unknown what he dies of but, fifty years later, the diary of John Ward, the vicar of Holy Trinity Church in Stratford (where Shagspere is buried) reports that *"Shakespeare, Drayton, and Ben Jonson had a merry meeting, and it seems drank too hard, for Shakespeare died of a fever there contracted."* Could he have been poisoned? I prefer to think he died of natural causes, but the timing did work out perfectly for Jonson.

Jonson's own folio (which precedes Shakespeare's) is a unique, major work and catapults him to literary stardom. He is allowed to become a Protestant again, receives a pension of £66/yr and is made the first Poet Laureate. The price is right!

In order to carry out his bargain with the Pembroke brothers, he starts work as chief editor of the giant book we call THE FIRST FOLIO containing thirty-six plays, 18 of which are appearing in print for the first time.

He plants the seeds of the upcoming Shakespeare Fraud in his own WORKS by including cast lists for EVERYMAN OUT OF HIS HUMOUR and SEJANUS, putting William Shakespeare at the top of the list in EVERYMAN, and spelling it with a hyphen and two capital "S's" ("Shake-Speare") in SEJANUS while putting it in the middle of the list. Shagspere now has three theatrical credits.

Jonson has help from several people with differing motives:

> Susan Vere—Oxford's youngest daughter: Thought to be one of the "grand possessors" who provided the scripts. I believe she is trying to collect and rescue her father's writing before it gets scattered and lost to posterity.

> Elizabeth Trentham (before she died in 1612)— Oxford's second wife who was trying to salvage what she could of Oxford's heritage and works. She was probably one of the "grand possessors" mentioned in the 1609 quarto of TROILUS AND CRESSIDA.

> Susan Vere's husband, Philip Herbert, Earl of Montgomery: Gentleman of the Privy Chamber, and dedicatee of The First Folio, wants to make sure the upcoming succession to Prince Charles goes smoothly by squelching underground rumors of Southampton-as-Tudor Prince. He can help his wife at the same time. He and his brother probably provide funds.

> Susan Vere's brother-in-law, William Herbert, 3rd Earl of Pembroke: An early favorite of King James (who served as Lord Chamberlain from 1615-1625), a dedicatee of The First Folio and, like his brother, is mostly interested in having a peaceful succession, but

it's nice to do something for his sister-in-law.

John Hemings and Henry Condell, actors with The Chamberlain's Men. The presence of these two men is Jonson's attempt to provide acting company bona fides for Shagspere. Why did they allow Jonson to use their names and pretend they actually did something to preserve the plays? What was in it for them? Besides the 26 Shillings, 8 Pence they each received through William Shagspere's will, I have no idea. Maybe that was enough.

The plays themselves vary in accuracy and completeness but I'm sure Jonson uses the best versions he has access to. The preface (the first 16 pages) however, is a different story. His assigned task is to give Shakespeare a face and a life and to make it appear that he was an actor who was born and raised in Stratford-on-Avon, a small sheep/wool center on the Avon River.

He dutifully carries out this task—except that he sabotages it. He seems to be walking a fine line between pleasing the powers that be and providing clues so a close reader can discover the truth.

Katherine Chiljan, in her book, *Shakespeare Suppressed,* has a fascinating chapter on "The First Folio Fraud" which I encourage you to read. According to Chiljan, Jonson got John Heminge and Henry Condell, actors, to claim that they were the collectors and guardians of the plays and to dedicate the book to the Pembroke brothers, Lords William and Phillip. In this dedication they use language and images taken from the classical writers Pliny and Horace. Heminges and Condell were neither writers nor scholars, but Jonson was a classical scholar and a writer. It appears that he wrote their dedications for them.

Heminge's and Condell's second letter *"To the great*

Variety of Readers" "*is a pastiche of phrases found in several of Jonson's works that are too many for coincidence.*" (Chiljan)

I have only one personal elaboration to add to her discussion: Jonson hires Martin Droeshout, an experienced professional artist, to do the engraving of Shakespeare to put on the title page. Droeshout draws a picture that historians have been arguing over for 400 years. He has taken a lot of flack for his incompetence but I believe that what he drew was intentionally created to Jonson's specifications. We often refer to the drawing in the front of the First Folio as a portrait of Shakespeare. What he actually drew might better be called Shakespeare's Mask.

Please refer to the enclosed drawing and note the following oddities:

1. The face, although apparently middle-aged is smooth and without lines.
2. The expression is incredibly bland and lifeless and appears mask-like.
3. The only life-like thing about the face is the eyes, which are looking directly at us.
4. There is a definite line extending down from his left ear and disappearing under the chin, which looks like the edge of a mask.
5. The head is too large for the body and appears to be floating above it on a sort of platter. It usually is called a ruff, but it is definitely not a ruff. It has been referred to by Stratfordian Charles Nicholl as a "stiff, tray-like collar."
6. This platter is in the shape of a shield. (There is a website which has a discussion of this shield. Shakespeare.info/William-shakespeare-collar-theory.htm)

7. The costume does not appear to have a real body inside it and certainly not his body, which, based on the size of his head, would be too big for the clothes. In fact, since it has been made with two left sleeves, (On the viewer's right is the left sleeve seen from the front. On the viewer's left is the left sleeve seen from the back) it would be impossible for a person to get into it. It appears to be an empty costume—no body inside.

I believe that what we are looking at is an engraving of a theatrical mask hiding a man's head without a body. The

mask has fake hair attached. The man's eyes are looking out at us through the eye-holes. The head is sitting on a platter shaped like a shield. ***Oxford is looking at us from behind a mask.***

If you'll remember, in Jonson's EVERY MAN OUT OF HIS HUMOUR, Sogliardo's coat of arms is the body of a boar without a head. (Oxford without the creative part). We are looking at the missing head served up on a platter just like boar's heads were traditionally served up on banquet trays at that time. This is a great Ben Jonson joke. I'll bet the "insiders" at the Mermaid Tavern fell on the floor laughing when they saw it. Admitting how ridiculous it looks, Jonson, on the page opposite the drawing says, "Reader, looke not on his Picture but his Booke." He is saying to us, "The contents of this book, the creation of his brilliant mind, is the most important thing to know about William Shakespeare. He's here but I'm not allowed to show you the face behind the mask." The academic world didn't get the joke and took Jonson at his word. The almost-official theatrical response to any question concerning authorship is, "It doesn't matter who wrote them as long as we have the works."

THE FIRST FOLIO is a great success. Cecil's version of history becomes the only version and no one, until Thomas Looney in 1919, ever re-connected Shakespeare and Oxford. Unfortunately, tradition won out over research and College professors all over the English speaking world still insist that the man who wrote the plays was a journeyman actor who lived in Stratford-on-Avon and whose father made leather gloves. Almost everyone has drunk the Kool-Aid. Our only consolation is to know that we have all been taken in by a master con artist, and we have lots of company.

Here we are, four centuries after the fact, and hardly anyone believes that Shakespeare was the Lord Great Chamberlain of England and father of a bastard prince who had the right, by blood, to succeed his mother, Elizabeth I, on the throne when she died. This is because of the giant fraud perpetrated by Robert Cecil to cover up the fact that he stole the English crown from a Tudor Prince of Elizabeth's blood and gave it to the Stuart King James VI of Scotland.

Hamlet:

O God, Horatio, what a wounded name,
Things standing thus unknown, shall leave behind me!
If thou didst ever hold me in thy heart,
Absent thee from felicity awhile
And in this harsh world draw thy breath in pain
To tell my story

Every time I read Hamlet's plea I think of Oxford and renew my resolve to try to tell his story. If you know a different complete story which is both logical and possible, please share it. Only through trying over and over again to tell a complete, coherent story will we finally end up at the total truth. Sartre tells us in *No Exit* that a man is not really dead as long as we're still thinking about him and talking about him. Shakespeare still lives, and we must rediscover his story.

BIBLIOGRAPHY

GPV Akrigg. *Shakespeare & the Earl of Southampton.* Cambridge, MA : Harvard University Press, 1968.

Percy Allen. *The Case for Edward de Vere, Seventeenth Earl of Oxford as "Shakespeare."* London : Cecil Palmer, 1930.

Robert Brazil. *The True Stoy of the Shake-speare Publications Vol 1.* (1999).

Katherine Chiljan. *Shakespeare Suppressed : The Uncensored Truth about Shakespeare and his Works.* San Francisco : Faire Editions, 2011.

Eva Turner Clark. *Hidden Allusions in Shakespeare's Plays.* New York : The Stratford Press, 1931.

Mary Hill Cole. *The Portable Queen.* Amherst : University of Massachusetts Press, 1999.

Valorie Fildes. *Wet-Nursing : A history from Antiquity to the present.* Oxford, New York : Basil Blackmell, 1988.

John Guy. *Elizabeth : The Forgotten Years.* New York : Viking, 2016.

Christopher Haigh. *Elizabeth I, Profiles in Power.* London : Routledge, 1988.

Paul E. J. Hammer. *Elizabeth's Wars : War, Government and Society in Tudor England*. New York : Palgrave Macmillan, 2003.

Paul E.J. Hammer. *The Polarisation of Elizabethan Politics : The Political Career of Robert Devereux, 2nd Earl of Essex, 1585-1597.* Cambridge, New York : Cambridge University Press, 1999.

Paul E.J. Hammer. "Shakespeare's Richard II, the Play of 7 February 1601, and the Essex Rising." *Shakespeare Quarterly*, Vol 59, No. 1, Spring 2008.

Robert Lacey. *Robert, Earl of Essex : An Elizabethan Icarus.* London : Phoenix Press, 1971.

J. Thomas Looney. *"Shakespeare" Identified in Edward de Vere, the Seventeenth Earl of Oxford.* London, New York : Frederick A. Stokes, 1920.

Scott McMillin & Sally-Beth MacLean. *The Queen's Men and their Plays.* Cambridge, New York : Cambridge University Press, 1998.

Charlton Ogburn, Jr. *The Mysterious William Shakespeare : The Myth and the Reality.* New York : Dodd, Mead, 1984.

Diana Price. *Shakespeare's Unorthodox Biography.* Westport, Conn. : Greenwood Press, 2001.

Alan Gordon Smith. *William Cecil, The Power Behind Elizabeth.* Honolulu, HI : University Press of the Pacific, 2004.

Charlotte Carmichael Stopes. *The Life of Henry, Third Earl of Southampton : Shakespeare's Patron.* Cambridge : Cambridge University Press, 1922.

Lytton Strachey. *Elizabeth and Essex.* New York : Harcourt, 1928.

B.M. Ward. *The Seventeenth Earl of Oxford.* London : John Murray, 1928.

Anna Whitelock. *The Queen's Bed.* New York : Farrar, Straus & Giroux 2013.

Hank Whittemore. *The Monument.* Marshfield, MA : Meadow Geese Press, 2005.

Hank Whittemore. *Twelve Years in the Life of Shakespeare.* Somerville, MA : Forever Press, 2012.

Hank Whittemore & Ted Story. *Shake-speare's Treason (A performance script).* New York, 2008.

Made in the USA
Middletown, DE
21 July 2016